A NEW SPIRIT IN PAINTING, 1981:

On Being an Antimodern

AF618910

Théo de Luca

Koenig Books, London

For my mother, Anne de Luca

CONTENTS

ACKNOWLEDGEMENTS

The origins of this book lie in a conference I attended in Paris in the spring of 2017. On that occasion, one of the speakers heavily and gratuitously criticised 'A New Spirit in Painting'. I thought such a violent reaction was dubious insofar as it was founded on categorical and flat statements. There is no catechism in arts, and for this reason, such criticism propelled me to do further research on the exhibition. Little did I know that my new curiosity would happen upon me the greatest possible pleasure: the unexpected reunion of some of the artists I grew up admiring. The second decisive moment happened a few months later, when I first met with Hans Ulrich Obrist thanks to María Inés Rodriguez, who taught me the making of exhibitions. He encouraged me to keep on working on this project and introduced me to Sir Norman Rosenthal. From that moment onwards, my research progressively evolved into this book.

During the writing of this manuscript, I had the chance to undertake a Grand Tour structured around the history of painting of the 1970s, in an age when displacements seem to be governed by the quest for the most exotic place. While based in London, Paris, and Bordeaux, I have shaped this project travelling to Berlin, Cologne, Dessau, Düsseldorf, Frankfurt, Märkisch Wilmersdorf, Stuttgart, Basel, Lausanne, Montreux, Rossinière, Zürich, Trieste, Venice, Barcelona, Edinburgh, Glasgow, New York City, Philadelphia, Baltimore, Washington, DC, New Canaan, Princeton and New Haven. These travels were essential for the development of my thinking: they allowed me to genuinely see the artworks which nurtured my essay.

First of all, I would like to thank the outstanding individuals with whom I conversed as I was preparing this book: Georg Baselitz, Rainer Fetting, Sir Norman Rosenthal, Sir Nicholas Serota, Jean-Louis Froment, Tim Marlow, Hans Ulrich Obrist, Anthony d'Offay, Thaddaeus Ropac and

Michael Werner. They all have generously supported me in many ways and I am infinitely grateful for their trust.
I am also indebted to Briony Fer for being the most forward-thinking, creative, honest and attentive mentor I could hope for. I would like to place this book under the sign of our conversations. I am equally indebted to another mentor, François-Marie Mourad, who has helped me shape my thought from the very beginning. They have both awakened my eye.
Three young and promising painters – Franziska Beilfuß, Sonya Derviz, Olivia Parkes – played a fundamental role in the bringing of this book into the world. They all gave me a hint of how real artists see the world and build a universe of their own.
For Franz König, my publisher, I have admiration as well as gratitude. I am also thankful to Nicole Rankers and Hanna Schmandin for their diligence and dedication as they were supervising the making of this book.
Moreover, this project could not have been possible without the invaluable support from: Harumi Klossowska de Rola; Richard Taws; Samo Gale from the Andy Warhol Foundation for the Visual Arts; Freddie Feilden and Marie-Louise Laband from Anthony d'Offay Ltd; Leeor Engländer, Detlev Gretenkort and Julia Westner from the Archiv Georg Baselitz; Yves Guignard from the Fonds Balthus; Lisa Bönig from the Büro Rainer Fetting; Cyril Chaumeau, Karine Daviaud, Pedro Jiménez Morrás and Béatrice Vigué from the CAPC musée d'art contemporain de Bordeaux; Sara Friedlander and Marv Recinto from Christie's; Eveline Schmid from the Daros Collection; Hanna Schouwink from David Zwirner; the Estate of Francis Bacon; the Estate of Philip Guston; the Estate of Robert Ryman; Silke Kellner-Mergenthaler from the Fondation Beyeler; Ellénita de Mol and Anne-Claire Duperrier from the Fundación Almine y Bernard Ruiz-Picasso para el Arte; Richard Calvocoressi and Lilias Wigan from Gagosian; Anders Bergstrom, Emily Rothrum and Graham Steele from Hauser & Wirth; Lorenz Ecker, Ariane Kossack and Anne Röhl who helped me prepare, conduct, transcribe and

translate the interview of Georg Baselitz; Birte Kleemann from the Michael Werner Gallery; Susan Dunne and Lindsay McGuire from the Pace Gallery; Jennifer Camilleri, Doireann Cott, Mark Pomeroy and Karine Sarant-Hawkins from the Royal Academy of Arts, London; Laura Macfarlane, Anh Nguyen and Laura Louise Norman from the Serpentine Galleries; Antonio Homem from the Sonnabend Gallery; Marja Bloem and Lauren van Haaften-Schick from the Stichting Egress Foundation; Laura Bertaux, Quentin Carvalho, Xenia Geroulanos, Lisa Mayr, Polly Robinson Gaer, Kristina Tencic and Xaver von Mentzingen from the Galerie Thaddaeus Ropac; Hetty Wessels from the Stedelijk Museum Amsterdam; Heidi Coleman and Amy Schichtel from the Willem de Kooning Foundation; the librarians of the Warburg Institute.

Above all, my thanks go to my friends, to my sister, Apolline de Luca, who beautifully gave a visual form to my work, to my brother, Timothée de Luca, to my father, Patrick de Luca, and to my grandfather, Bachir Khalef. Finally, I dedicate this book to my late mother, Anne de Luca, whose loss is felt everywhere and who is the person I constantly look forward to. She is the one who inspired my love for the arts, taking me, as a child, to museums around the world and to the studio she rented to make still life and Klee-like paintings after work.

ESSAY

'et que la peinture fût l'amante de la beauté et la reine de l'art'

'e la pittura vagheggiatrice della bellezza e Regina dell'arte'

'painting is the lover of beauty and queen of the arts'

'die Malerei ist die Geliebte der Schönheit und Königin der Künste'

Nicolas Poussin

A NEW SPIRIT IN PAINTING, 1981:

INTRODUCTION

> *L'Éléphant est le plus sage de tous les animaux, le seul qui se souvienne de ses vies antérieures; aussi se tient-il longtemps tranquille, méditant à leur sujet.*
>
> —Buddhist text[1]

Thirty-eight years later, 'A New Spirit in Painting' needs to be revisited. The exhibition, curated by Christos M. Joachimides, Norman Rosenthal and Nicholas Serota, crystallised at the Royal Academy of Arts in London the so-called "return" to figurative painting and the emergence of Neo-Expressionism, which both occurred in the 1970s. The exhibition was groundbreaking and set the art world agenda for the next decade but the opinion was however divided on whether it was seminal or not, to such an extent that many institutions ignored it. Most of today's art historians consider it as a "bad object" for two reasons: first, its seemingly provocative and reactionary nature; second, its lack of coherence as a whole – divergent painters were paired. Nonetheless, it cannot be said that the exhibition is not an art historical object in its own right since it is paradigmatic of what painting should be then for an apparently heterogeneous group of painters. The scope of this essay is not part of a history of exhibitions. Rather, it considers the historical moment the exhibition encapsulated. We can look back at it as one of the precipitates, the shots, or the sedimentary rocks produced by the 1970s: it provides the historian with an exemplary *vantage point* to tackle the debates around painting proper to that period.

The exhibition as well as the historical moment it embodied were criticised because of their set of claims,

---

[1] Quoted in Malraux, 1976, p. 1.

regarded as untenable since it reenacted aesthetic positions criticised and rejected by the end of the 1960s. Inasmuch as the artists' nationalities and regionalism were emphasised, the exhibition was said to stem from the "Old Masters" rhetoric. Three generations of artists were distinguished in order to convey a sense of a generational and genealogical phenomenon: the older generation (Balthus, Francis Bacon, Willem de Kooning, Philip Guston...), the middle generation (Georg Baselitz, Markus Lüpertz, Gerhard Richter, Robert Ryman, Cy Twombly, Andy Warhol...), the young generation (Anselm Kiefer, Rainer Fetting...).[2] Although the paintings were not systematically displayed in accordance with this generational logic, it was thought that Pablo Picasso was erected as the driving force of the recent "return" to painting since four of his late works were placed in the central hall of the Royal Academy. But one should remember that the late Picasso was far from being accepted then.

Subsequently, an agenda of exhibitions jointly organised or supervised by Joachimides and Rosenthal supported the institutional establishment of the two curators' narrative, which later achieved a European acceptance: 'Zeitgeist' (1982) at the Martin-Gropius-Bau in Berlin as well as 'German Art' (1985), 'British Art' (1987), 'Italian Art' (1989) and 'American Art in the Twentieth Century' (1993) at the Royal Academy in London. Moreover, the curators inscribed this historically localised phenomenon in the history of modern painting and "Great Art", invoking the Northern Expressionist tradition.[3] It can indeed be argued that such a legacy lies in those works but this argument can enlighten almost every postwar painterly attempt. Northern Expressionism was actually used to praise the paintings' expressive qualities – intense colours, acid forms, energetic visuality (think of Thomas Kirchner or George Grosz).

More than a "return" to figurative painting, the curators envisioned this new phase in the history of art

---

[2] See Joachimides, Rosenthal, Serota, *A New Spirit in Painting* (exh. cat.), 1981, p. 11; Joachimides, *A New Spirit in Painting* (exh. cat.), 1981, pp. 15, 16. See also List of the artists of 'A New Spirit in Painting' (2 October, 1980; 11 December, 1980), RAA/PRA/9/39, Royal Academy of Arts, London.
[3] Joachimides et al., 1981, p. 12.

as a “return” to the representation of human experiences, which was, according to them, prohibited in the 1960s. They thus justified the inclusion of abstract works in the exhibition, sometimes disregarding their meaning and instrumentalising their content.[4] The works were said to express the rediscovery of the private sphere. Self-expression was celebrated and the mythologised figure of “the artist” was recovered. Painting was thus assigned therapeutic and post-existentialist functions.[5] Rosenthal’s description of Markus Lüpertz’s dithyrambic paintings – for example, *Schwarz-Rot-Gold dythirambisch I* (Figure 1) – epitomised what was thought to be the curators’ reading:

> His paintings [...] are political assertions that confront, with irony, German motifs of this century, placing them in close proximity to the artist and his palette, and defining the artist in his defiant role as the only possible hero for our age. [...] The artists of the postwar period who perhaps best represent the German spirit are those who, taking the fullest cognisance of the horrors of this century, incorporate with both irony and respect a reverence for the healing powers of the artist and the resonant cultural tradition of Germany.[6]

In this text, postwar German art was interpreted in a deterministic way, mediated by German cultural tradition and driven by a consciousness of recent political events as

---

[4] *Ibid.*, p. 12: ‘There are outstanding non- figurative paintings in our exhibition. However, it is surely unthinkable that the representation of human experiences, in other words people and their emotions, landscapes and still-lives, could forever be excluded from painting. They must in the long run again return to the centre of the argument of painting. This is a central proposition of this exhibition.’

[5] See the emphatic vocabulary of Joachimides in Joachimides, 1981, pp. 14, 15, 16. For example: ‘This new concern with painting is related to a certain subjective vision, a vision that includes both an understanding of the artist himself as an individual engaged in a search for self-realisation and as an actor on the wider historical stage.’ See also Rosenthal, 1985, p. 13: ‘the concern is with art as a therapeutic activity, a means towards a better, more optimistic form of life.’

[6] Rosenthal, 1985, p. 20. For an account of the readings characteristic of the curators, critics and art historians who championed the *new spirit in painting*, see Buchloh, 1981 [especially pp. 64-68].

well as a Hegelian interpretation of Alois Riegl's *Kunstwollen*, which is rather embedded in Zarathustra's vital force.[7] The works' formal qualities were understood in that light and only described in stereotypical terms. Their intrinsic meaning was not acknowledged inasmuch as the works' main properties are not linked to postwar history, but rather lie in the painterly language they play out. The criteria which underpinned the so-called 'affinities' between the painters brought together remained however vague and elusive: 'intensity', 'an obsessive interest in what painting can communicate' and 'direct stylistic comparisons'.[8] The very elements enabling these stylistic comparisons were neither elaborated nor were they clarified.

The critics who championed the *new spirit in painting* in the 1970s and 1980s (Rudi Fuchs, Siegfried Gohr or Donald Kuspit) emphasised the same political aspects described above. No alternative interpretations reaching an international audience were proposed. Penetrating observations were however formulated by less well-known stakeholders. For example, Jean-Louis Froment challenged the dominant views of that period, organising an array of exhibitions at the CAPC, in Bordeaux. One could think of 'Légendes' (1984), in which artists such as Pablo Picasso, Andy Warhol and Georg Baselitz revolved around extracts from Michel de Montaigne's *Essais*.[9]

In sum, the curators who pushed Neo-Expressionism to the art world's centre were those who, at least partly, embraced the so-called new-spirit theoretical apparatus. Therefore, it was mistakenly thought that most of the works from 'A New Spirit in Painting' hinged on the characteristics noted above – that is why much art critics responded to the exhibition with violence. They thought it was an art-world phenomenon and criticised what was regarded as a regression: the arguments which had once been directed against Abstract Expressionism and Clement Greenberg could be directed against the "return" to figurative painting. In this regard, Lucy Lippard's critique of formalism in 1976 could have been

---

[7] Rosenthal, 1985, p. 17. On the concept of *Kunstwollen*, see Panofsky, 1981 and Kaschnitz-Weinberg, 2016.
[8] Joachimides et al., 1981, p. 11.
[9] *Légendes* (exh. cat.), 1984, pp. 35-41.

against the rhetoric of 'A New Spirit in Painting':

> I recognised now the seeds of feminism in my revolt against Clement Greenberg's patronisation of artists [...], against the 'masterpiece' syndrome, the 'three great artists' syndrome and so forth.[10]

Further arguments against the "return" to figurative painting included: the 'huge canvas', the 'heavy frame', the 'grand style', the 'very heavy thematics' and the masculine painterly gestures syndromes.[11]

For much critics, Neo-Expressionism and its derivatives were postmodern art – that is to say eclectic, pluralist, a mishmash of styles. Consequently, the exhibition was absorbed by the modern/postmodern debate soon after its opening. The epitome of the reaction against Neo-Expressionism is to be found in Benjamin Buchloh's 'Figures of Authority, Ciphers of Regression', published in *October* in the spring of 1981 and presented at the Vancouver Conference on Modernism in March 1981 – which was attended by Clement Greenberg as well as the upholders of the social history of art (Timothy J. Clark, Thomas E. Crow). For Buchloh, the *new spirit in painting* was driven by the market, achieved the commodification of painting and reflected the neoconservative ideology characteristic of Thatcherism and Ronald Reagan's presidency.

Donald Kuspit, one of the few advocates of Neo-Expressionism in America, responded directly to Buchloh. However, Kuspit's criticism was sometimes uncritical: he ignored the paintings' pictoriality and his judgment relied almost exclusively on the works' historical background. Works were indeed understood as mere illustrations of historical events (e.g. post-Nazi Germany for German painters).[12] Such a reading – based on the assumption that the Second World War

---

[10] Lippard, 1976, p. 3 quoted in Dubreuil-Blondin, 1983, pp. 195-211.

[11] See Kozloff, 1974, p. 40; Buchloh, 1981, p. 58; Foster, 1985, p. 76.

[12] See Kuspit, 1982 and Kuspit, 1983. For a summary of the discussions about painting and modernism condensed by the debate between Buchloh and Kuspit, see Krens in *Refigured Painting: The German Image 1960-88* (exh. cat.), 1989.

and the Holocaust are the two traumatic events that foreground the whole history of postwar western arts – appealed to many art historians and critics. In this respect, painters who were not Neo-Expressionist but associated with the *new spirit in painting* were thought to respond to this postwar historical logic – think of the way the red armband bearing a swastika in Francis Bacon's *Crucifixion* (1965) has been tackled.[13]

But the critics against 'A New Spirit in Painting' solely picked up on remarks which allowed them to attack and turn down a challenge they could not accept. Yet Joachimides, Rosenthal and Serota acknowledged characteristics which did justice to the artists and their works – one could think of the text Serota wrote for the Anselm Kiefer exhibition jointly organised by the Whitechapel Gallery and the Museum Folkwang in 1981.[14] However, no real theoretical apparatus underpinned 'A New Spirit in Painting'. This attitude ran counter to the period's tendency to theorise and survey the state of the art through international art exhibitions.[15] The absence of theory is precisely what gave 'A New Spirit in Painting' a sense of urgency, and makes it so vital and fresh, still today. Artworks were not shadowed. They have survived the taste of time and now speak for themselves.

Today, it seems legitimate to reassess the "return" to figurative painting beyond the mere binary and Manichean debates between modernism and postmodernism, figuration and abstraction, (neo)avantgarde and academism, neoclassicism, or neoconservatism, masculinity and femininity. We should remember that many women artists also painted in a Neo-Expressionist vein at the time (think of Susan Rothenberg's *Butterfly* from the NGA or Marlene Dumas's and Maria Lassnig's self-portraits).

Moreover, we cannot confine ourselves to the *new spirit in painting* should we like to reconfigure boldly the narrative

---

[13] Sylvester, 1987, p. 65 and Sylvester in *Willem de Kooning* (exh. cat.), 1994, p. 27.
[14] Serota in Anselm Kiefer (exh. cat.), 1981, pp. 19-23.
[15] In Europe, one could think of the exhibitions Kasper König curated in Cologne and Düsseldorf such as 'Westkunst' (1981) or 'Von hier aus' (1984). In the US, one could think of 'Endgame', which involved most of the protagonists from *October* in 1986 at the Institute of Contemporary Art in Boston.

of the "return" to painting. Such a phenomenon was neither a *coup de théâtre* nor was it a repetition of, say, the *retour à l'ordre*. What was intertwined with the emergence of the *new spirit* needs to be identified in order to legitimise the pairing of the so-called Neo-Expressionists with older painters such as Picasso, Bacon or Guston. Building upon these remarks, I will endeavour to show what is penetrating today in 'A New Spirit in Painting' and to what extent is postmodernism an inadequate concept for Neo-Expressionism. But we need to find, in the first instance, a model to extract from history the elements necessary to a comprehensive understanding of what was really at stake in the "return" to painting.

In 1977, Hubert Damisch proposed to consider Abstract Expressionism as part of a game of chess, spanning from the 1950s to the 1960s.[16] For Damisch, the art historian willing to reconstruct the game 'Painting' *after-the-fact* (regardless of the period) has to choose wisely the pieces he or she includes as well as their position on the chessboard.[17] He thus supported the establishment of a history of art which is not subordinated to historical time but is formed of discontinuities.[18] He argued for a history of art whose origin lies in artworks, without neglecting their historical nature. This model resonates with Walter Benjamin's hypotheses on the reassessment of historical materialism:

---

[16] Damisch, 1984, pp. 142-179. Damisch explored further the idea of the game of chess (which he likely borrowed from Marcel Duchamp) as a model for the history of art through an exhibition he curated in 1997 at the Museum Boymans Van Beuningen in Rotterdam: 'Moves: Playing Chess and Cards with the Museum'. Damisch also wrote an article about Duchamp's lifelong interest in chess, in which he compared painting with chess (insofar as they are both *cosa mentale*) and investigated chess as a paradigm for the analysis of Duchamp's oeuvre (see Damisch, 1979). The game of chess might be an exemplary model to describe the artistic creation: it is a transformative plastic construction. As Duchamp put it: 'all artists are not chess players, all chess players are artists.'

[17] Damisch, 1984, pp. 157-158.

[18] *Ibid.*, pp. 178-179. The origins of this idea can be found in Aby Warburg's conception of history (for a definition, see Didi-Huberman, 1999-2000, p. 227). The need to clearly define the concept of history was one the central issues raised by the modern/postmodern debate; see Marcelin Pleynet's remarks in the concluding panel discussion of the Vancouver Conference on Modernism in *Modernism and Modernity*, 1983, p. 273.

> A central problem of historical materialism that ought to be seen in the end: Must the Marxist understanding of history necessarily be acquired at the expense of the perceptibility of history? [...] The first stage in this undertaking will be to carry over the principle of montage into history (*das Prinzip der Montage*). That is, to assemble large-scale constructions out of the smallest and most precisely cut components. Indeed, to discover in the analysis of the small individual moment (*Einzelmoments*) the crystal of the total event. And, therefore, to break with vulgar historical naturalism. To grasp the construction of history as such.[19]

Benjamin's small individual moments resonate with Damisch's chess pieces. Both thinkers consider history in terms of visuality and visibility. The fact that Benjamin urges the historian to select specific events to reach the essence of a given historical moment is crucial. Regarding the "return" to figurative painting, the real issue is what are the individual moments, or, the chess pieces (or, the artworks), necessary to discover the crystal of the total event, or, the nature of the chessboard? How did figurative painting stand out in the 1970s? Was the "return" to painting a mere regression? Can we identify today an Ariadne's thread that leads to a narrative allowing to gain new perspectives on the *new spirit in painting*?

The three sets of chess pieces I would like to integrate to the chessboard modeling the party 'Painting' in the 1970s are: first, 1970s figurative painting, second, Conceptual art, third, Abstract Expressionism. The three parties can be regarded as strands forming a plait, as in a plait of hair or a plait of rope as described by Hubert Damisch.[20] One can find in 1970s figurative painting the inverted definition of Conceptual art, and vice versa, as much as one can find in Conceptual art the inverted definition of Abstract Expressionism and vice versa.

---

[19] Benjamin, 1999, p. 461. For an analysis of this passage, see Didi-Huberman, 1992, pp. 147-148. As noted by Didi-Huberman, the notion of montage echoes Sergei Eisenstein's film theory of montage and cubism collage. This process is also related to Claude Lévi-Strauss' structuralist method which is partly derived from Max Ernst's collages (Lévi-Strauss, 1983, pp. 327-328).
[20] See Damisch, 1984.

THE 1970s PLAIT:

PAINTING RECONFIGURED

I

After the Sovereignty of Conceptual art

I wanted to get away from the physical aspect of painting. I was much more interested in recreating ideas in painting [...] not merely in visual products.

—Marcel Duchamp[21]

Conceptual art is arguably the antithesis of the *new spirit in painting*. Yet, it fed into the history of painting to develop its own language. Henry Flint first coined the term in 'Concept art', which was published in 1961:

> "Concept art" is first of all an art of which the material is "concepts" [...] [and] language.[22]

Flynt's definition coincided with a revival of Duchampian tactics, which were directed against a purely retinal art. But Duchamp was not against painting per se nor did he obliterate painting. He rather expanded the pictorial conceptualising the ready-made. This is one reason why he was 'sick of the expression 'bête comme un peintre' – stupid as a painter.'[23] When referring to a purely retinal art, Duchamp did not declare himself against painting's visuality, he declared himself against realism.[24] He thus criticised the painters blindly enthusiastic about the immediacy of what the

[21] Duchamp in Sweeney, 1946, p. 20.
[22] Flynt, 1963.
[23] Duchamp in Sweeney, 1946, p. 21
[24] de Duve, 2014, p. 43

eye (or the camera) sees. For Duchamp, their own failure was a caricatural sensuality and physicality as much as the loss of painting's ability to convey ideas.[25] There has since been an orthodoxy of Duchamp's sayings. In the 1960s, they were misunderstood and instrumentalised to counter high modernism's beliefs. But "the withdrawal of visuality"[26] – paired with a cold nominalism – was not the only way out and proved to be a dead-end. Conceptual artists nonetheless developed an art without object, whose matter is language, in order to abandon the artwork's visual qualities.[27] Lucy Lippard and John Chandler epitomised this attitude in 1967, writing 'The Dematerialisation of Art'.[28] They heavily criticised formalism and Abstract Expressionism, arguing that the notion of object (read: painting) had become obsolete.[29] Moreover, Conceptual artists' attacks on painting involved a critique of the classical forms and practices of the exhibition: painting foolishly required the museum to be shown and seen. The artists who redefined the exhibition framework gravitated around the American gallerist Seth Siegelaub, who conceptualised the exhibitions-as-books. In 1968, he edited *Douglas Huebler, November 1968* (the first catalogue which was exhibition in itself) and launched *Xerox Book* after having invited seven artists (Carl Andre, Robert Barry, Douglas Huebler, Joseph

[25] See Duchamp in Sweeney, 1946, p. 20: 'In fact until the last hundred years all painting had been literary or religious: it had all been at the service of the mind. This characteristic was lost little by little during the last century. The more sensual appeal a painting provided – the more animal it became – the more highly it was regarded.'

[26] Crow, 1996, p. 213

[27] ...and perhaps Conceptual artists underestimated the power of painting to represent an idea. See Panofsky, 1924, p. 17 for a definition of Neoplatonic aesthetics, to which Panofsky was drawn (think of the two last chapters of his *Studies on Iconology* about Bandinelli, Titian and Michelangelo): 'Die ästhetische Anschauung des Neuplatonismus [...], die in jeder Erscheinungsform des Schönen nur das unzureichende Symbol einer nächsthöheren Erscheinungsform desselben erblickt, sodaß die sichtbare Schönheit gleichsam nur den Reflex einer unsichtbaren, und diese wiederum nur den Reflex der absoluten darstellt.' Although the ability to express an Idea through sensible forms is characteristic of classical representation, now it seems that one of the artist's tasks is to express the trace of this Idea (that is to say its demise), as it will be shown in this essay. See Nancy, 2001, pp. 133-160.

[28] Lippard, Chandler, 1968, pp. 31-36.

[29] See, for example, Robert Morris's remark in 1967, quoted in Buchloh, 2000, p. 560: 'The mode of painting has become antique.'

Kosuth, Sol LeWitt, Robert Morris, Lawrence Weiner) to each create a twenty-five-page work using photocopy.[30]

For these three reasons – first, Conceptual artists' refusal of the visual quality of art, second, their will to obliterate the object, third, their dismissal of the traditional forms of the exhibition – we can say that Conceptual art is the opposite of the "return" to figurative painting. For example, 'A New Spirit in Painting' played upon an array of elements radically rejected by Conceptual artists: works were gilded framed, hung on Hessian walls, in a Palladian mansion et cetera.

Yet, as noted by Benjamin Buchloh, the fact that 'the first poster Weiner produced [...] announces an exhibition of his paintings at the Seth Siegelaub Gallery in New York, in 1965', shows 'that reflection on painting [...] also formed the basis of [...] Conceptual art.'[31] In 1981 Buchloh suggested two criteria – originally used to criticise Neo-Expressionism and to describe Richter's, Ryman's and Stella's paintings – which could be applied to a comparative analysis of Conceptual art and "figurative" painting: coded, as opposed to uncoded, and mediated, as opposed to unmediated.[32] "Figurative" painting could be regarded as uncoded and unmediated whereas Conceptual art could be regarded as coded and mediated. Similarly, when Harald Szeemann conceptualised *documenta 5*[33], he argued that figurative painting was the representation of reality and that Conceptual art was congruent to reality.[34] What is at stake in this opposition – beyond its reductive and simplistic nature – is the evidence that Conceptual art and figurative painting gave shape to a plait, in Hubert Damisch's sense of the word, as much as Conceptual art formed another plait with Abstract Expressionism when the former originated in the 1960s.[35]

The interrelationship between figurative painting and

---

[30] See Bourel in *Art conceptuel I* (exh. cat.), 1988, p. 11.
[31] Buchloh, 2000, p. 558.
[32] Buchloh, 1981, p. 56, 58.
[33] Although this documenta was predominantly conceptual, it also included works by the so-called Neo-Expressionists such as Baselitz or Penck.
[34] Ammann, Brock, Szeemann, 2007, p. 97.
[35] See note 20 above.

Conceptual art became stronger in the mid-1970s because of the "return" to painting. From that moment on, Conceptual art entered into a new phase of its history as Thomas McEvilley has shown.[36] Several Conceptual artists even created works based on the permutation of parameters specific to the paintings they criticised (think of Art & Language). In a way, Conceptual art is the *enfant terrible* of painting since it sought to undermine the pictorial.

I would like to consider two artists whose works produced throughout that period shed light on the position of Conceptual art with regard to painting: Lawrence Weiner and the art group Art & Language. They frame the 1970s but also embody two contrasting aesthetic attitudes derived from painting. Lawrence Weiner worked towards the migration of painting – or, to speak like Hubert Damisch, towards a radical *displacement* of the notion of painting[37], while Art & Language worked within the boundaries of painting from the second half of the 1970s onwards.

FROM LAWRENCE WEINER...

For Benjamin Buchloh, Weiner's posters can be compared with analytic cubism and a post-Mallamarmean realm since his linguistic operations are based on pictorial and sculptural conventions. Like the cubists, he used language for its value per se (not for its poetological value), in order to elaborate a syntagmatic conception of the artwork and to contest the supremacy of the pictorial.[38] Buchloh exemplified his comparison quoting a passage from Apollinaire's 'Zone', in which the French poet claims that poetry now lies in flyers, catalogues and hoardings.[39]

But there might be another work by Apollinaire which

---

[36] McEvilley, 1985. For an account of the renewed interest in painting in the 1970s from an American formalist perspective, see Crimp, 1981.
[37] See Damisch, 'La déplacée' in Damisch, 2016, pp. 217-231. *Displacement* is also a word Weiner used to describe his own practice; see *Displacement* (exh. cat.), 1991.
[38] See Buchloh, 2000, pp. 556, 559.
[39] *Ibid.*, p. 555, 556.

reflects better how language progressively incorporated the pictorial and consequently assumed the role of painting in the rise of modernity: 'Cœur, Couronne et Miroir' – originally published in *Calligrammes* in 1918 (Figure 2).[40] I would like to focus on the mirror. The text that surrounds the words 'Guillaume' and 'Apollinaire' produces an image and reflects it. Nonetheless, this reflection is not, strictly speaking, the image of the subject, but the symptom or the *clue*[41] of this very subject. The text indicates the relationship between the subject and the pictorial dispositif: 'je suis enclos' (I am enclosed). In other words, the text frames the subject. In this regard, Apollinaire's 'Miroir' can be compared with Nicolas Poussin's *Paysage de tempête avec Pyrame et Thisbé* (Figure 3). The lake in the Poussinian landscape is not reflexive but reflective, the viewer's eye can be reflected to become the painting's reflection, or, the reflection on painting.[42] The figures around the lake are the parerga, like the text around 'Guillaume Apollinaire'. As such, the frame is deictic as it points out the painting's space of presentation.[43]

In 1969, *36" X 36" Removal to the Lathing or Support Wall of Plaster or Wallboard from a Wall* (Figure 4) played out specular effects similar to Poussin's and Apollinaire's works. The empty surfaces outlined by the squares cut from everyday materials produced the same kind of dialectical and dialogical exchanges between the inside and the outside. However, the modernist square was paired with the contingency of the environment in which it was inscribed (in that case, the exhibition 'When Attitudes Become Form'). Weiner actually stipulated that the work's dimensions are variable and that the medium is 'the language and the materials referred to.' The work is reproducible and ever-changing: its volatility jeopardises its own closure. Weiner thus abandoned arbitrariness, inviting the audience to modulate the work's parameters, and criticised the art object's traditional features, that is to say the notions of authorship and ownership, which rely on the object as

[40] Apollinaire, 1918, p. 56.
[41] See Ginzburg, 1980.
[42] See Marin, 1981.
[43] See Marin, 1988 [especially pp. 67-68].

a commodity.[44]

According to the logic of the avant-garde, the fact that traditional forms of painting were regarded as obsolete in the late 1960s may be partly explained by the work of an artist like Weiner – who was after all a painter, insofar as he 'continue[d] to expand [the] emphasis on gestural rigour and procedural immediacy, as much as they focus on the physicality of painterly procedures.'[45] However, Conceptual art became orthodox in the 1970s and showed the first signs of decline, which were accompanied by another kind of "return" to the pictorial, symptomatic of the reconfiguration of painting.[46]

...TO ART & LANGUAGE

Art & Language had engaged with the high genres of art throughout the 1960s and incorporated painting in their practice throughout the 1970s. In doing so, they sought to criticise Neo-Expressionism and to distance themselves from Conceptual art's *theoretical aura*[47] and orthodoxy.[48]

Art & Language criticised the hype around reflections on the human condition, writing 'On the Recent Fashion for Caring' in 1979.[49] In 1981, they turned post-existentialist concerns into a parody authoring a metaphysical and psychological description of a painting they achieved the same year. But these pieces are embedded in the *discours* (as described by Michel Foucault) triggered by the works Art & Language criticised. At the same time, they produced a series of paintings which is perhaps more consistent to capture the *Zeitgeist* of the 1970s.

Attacked by an Unknown Man in City Park: A Dying Woman: Drawn and Painted by Mouth is commonly interpreted as a work that symbolises the return of machismo in the art

---

[44] Buchloh, 2000, p. 564, 571, 572-574.
[45] *Ibid.*, p. 563.
[46] See note 33 above.
[47] Dubreuil-Blondin, 1983, note 8, p. 211.
[48] Harrison, 1991, pp. 156, 157.
[49] *Ibid.*, note 8, p. 280.

world because of its pornography.[50] It is nonetheless crucial to notice that Art & Language detailed the technique they used: 'painted by mouth'. Whether it was really painted by mouth is not important. Art & Language were ironically referring to Neo-Expressionists, whom often painted with their fingers instead of their brushes (think of Baselitz's *Fingermalerei*) and thus investigated an ancient technique – Michelangelo partly painted the Sistine Chapel with his fingers, to name but one.

The Studio at 3 Wesley Place might be Art & Language's most exemplary work with regard to the contemporary debates around painting. This work quotes Courbet's *Artist's Studio*, which is represented on the table at the left-hand side, under a reproduction of Manet's *Olympia*. However, *Studio at 3 Wesley Place* does not function like Courbet's work. The latter is the strict representation of Courbet's oeuvre and aesthetic programme whereas the former is an eccentric and schizophrenic myriad of references. In total, over sixty references are quoted (paintings, books, persons...).[51] This is one reason why the work can be regarded as the parodic representation of what could be a Neo-Expressionist studio in the 1970s since pluralism was said to be Neo-Expressionism's characteristic strategy.[52]

For Charles Harrison, Art & Language actually pursued painting to recover mannerism and gain opacity.[53] It might indeed be argued that Art & Language painted mannerist works to criticise the "return" to painting. However, they did it with neither *sprezzatura* nor *bravura*.[54] As a result, the works were not delicate and exquisite, but eventually the product of bourgeois and amateur painterly practices. Inasmuch as *The Studio at 3 Wesley Place* can be considered as, say, a missed version of Johan Zofanny's *Tribuna of the Uffizi*, it looks like a mockery of connoisseurship, which was simulated by a stratum of the art world at the time.

---

[50] *Ibid.*, p. 163.
[51] *Ibid.*, p. 166 and note 25, p. 279.
[52] See 'Against Pluralism' in Foster, 1985, pp. 13-32.
[53] Harrison, 1991, p. 157.
[54] On *bravura* and *sprezzatura*, see Suthor, 2010. Especially 'IL BRAVO', pp. 25-36 and 'sprezzatura', pp. 87-96.

The trajectory of Conceptual art, from Lawrence Weiner to Art & Language, shows that the "return" to painting is a much more complex phenomenon than had been thought. It cannot be regarded as a mere capriccio provoked by the art market and its stakeholders. Indeed, it did not only set the agenda of the art world but also redefined the parameters of artistic creation in the course of the 1970s. We should thus take a closer look at the so-called figurative works painted throughout that decade. But let us remind ourselves that Conceptual art fed into Abstract Expressionism, and so did the *new spirit in painting*, despite the claim that it was impossible to paint figures after Jackson Pollock.

The Last Word Must Always Secretly Be the First: Remarks on Jackson Pollock and Ad Reinhardt

> *Modern Architecture is not a few branches from an old tree – it is a new growth coming right from the roots. [...] What we [look] for [is] a new approach not a new style.*
>
> —Walter Gropius[55]

> *When [...] you pick up something from an earlier period and adapt it to your own work an approach can be creative. The result is not new; but it is new insomuch as it is a different approach.*
>
> —Marcel Duchamp[56]

Abstract Expressionism is commonly associated with Clement Greenberg's modernism, whose aim was the purification of painting and the erasure of its expendables.[57] Jean-François Lyotard's description of Pollock's *Painting* (1948) illustrates the reasons why common narratives on modern and contemporary art argue that Abstract Expressionism historically put an end to painting, or, at least, to figurative painting:

---

[55] Gropius, 1962, p. 83.
[56] Duchamp in Sweeney, 1946, p. 19
[57] See Greenberg, Vol. 4, 1993, pp. 84-93.

> [...] plastic screen entirely covered by chromatic runs; absence of all line of construction, of all tracing even; disappearance of echo or rhythm effects produced by repetitions or recurrences of forms, values or colours on the painting's surface; indeed, elimination of all recognisable figure.[58]

However, Clement Greenberg had foreseen that his interpretation of Abstract Expressionism's historical and cultural momentum could shift. He had also understood that Pollock's works were not a rupture in the history of painting but rather a new point of departure.[59] Hence, I would like to investigate to what extent can it be argued that Pollock and Abstract Expressionism can be regarded as the seeds of the *new spirit in painting.*

It might be appealing to suggest a purely morphological interpretation of the links between Abstract Expressionism and Neo-Expressionism. Although Michael Fried would not advocate such an interpretation, his description of Pollock's black paintings could underpin it. For Fried, 'bare canvas areas gain in imagistic significance' and the black forms 'have their own specific, animistic character' in *Number 15* (1951).[60] Building on this remark, one could argue that the forms from Pollock's black paintings progressively metamorphosed into Neo-Expressionist figures. However, an analysis embedded in a vitalist or naturalist model, strictly borrowed from biology and based on the notion of "evolution", would be deterministic and would not do justice to the artists.[61] We should rather take a look at an exhibition which provided young European artists of the 1950s and the 1960s with an alternative to the École de Paris.

---

58 Lyotard, 2011, p. 275.

59 See Greenberg, Vol. 3, 1993, pp. 186-193. Especially pp. 192-193: '[...] the connoisseurs of the future may interpret representational as well as abstract painting in terms quite different from ours. [...] I do not feel that abstract painting, despite all the changes it has made in the language of painting, is so different from traditional, representational painting as to constitute a real historical break with it.'

60 Fried in *Pollock* (exh. cat.), 2015, p. 62.

61 See Focillon, 1947, p. 12.

In 1958, the International Programme of the Museum of Modern Art, New York organised 'The New American Painting'. The exhibition toured in eight European countries and was instigated by Alfred H. Barr, Jr. It included the works of all the major Abstract Expressionists. Young European artists were strongly influenced by the exhibition then, especially German painters as Baselitz later recalled.[62]

It should also be noted that the texts published in the exhibition catalogue resonate with the "return" to painting. In the introductory essay, Barr remarked that 'Pollock and de Kooning painted a number of pictures with recognisable figures, to the dismay of some of their followers who had been inclined to make an orthodoxy of abstraction.'[63] Moreover, André Chastel, whose review for the French newspaper *Le Monde* was part of the catalogue, wrote that 'the roots of [Abstract Expressionism] are European, and are called Fauvism, German Expressionism, Klee, Picasso [...].'[64] On the one hand, Barr stated that Pollock's works were not strictly abstract and that abstraction was by then orthodox, on the other, Chastel associated Pollock and his fellow painters with artists who were undeniable sources for Neo-Expressionism.

Hence, whether Barr's and Chastel's statements are true, we can suppose that Pollock's oeuvre was one of the very bases of much of Neo-Expressionist reflections. Neo-Expressionists' engagement with Pollock's works was neither a matter of institutionalisation, nor was it the assimilation of the New York School's pictorial language (as it has been argued by the postmodern critique).[65] They rather strove to develop a new approach derived from the pictorial issues formulated by Abstract Expressionism. It might even be said that the exhibition intimated that painting should start exploring other ways than abstraction. For example, *Number 27* (1951), one of Pollock's works included in 'The New American Painting', seems to have prepared the ground for the "return" to figurative painting. The recognisable figures

[62] Shiff, 2002, p. 54 and note 11, p. 109.
[63] Barr in *The New American Painting* (exh. cat.), 1959, p. 19.
[64] Chastel quoted in *The New American Painting* (exh. cat.), 1959, p. 13.
[65] Buchloh, 1981, p. 63.

in it can indeed be regarded as an alternative to the allovers.

In this regard, Pollock's late works are exemplary.[66] They either exhibit figures, as in *Number 27*, or hide figures, as in *The Deep* (Figure 5). In the latter, the white paint encircles a figure that is an empty form and resembles the silhouette of a mummy. It is as if the burial of the figure was depicted.[67] If Pollock buried the figure, maybe was it the task of a younger generation of painters to exhume the figure?

The American painter Ad Reinhardt would have probably answered to this question in the negative. From the end of the 1950s, he was 'just making the last paintings which anyone can make.'[68] Like Rodchenko, Reinhardt wanted to paint "the last painting". But he did not want to come to an end with painting since 'the paradox of his black paintings is that of an endless end.'[69] Ad Reinhardt rather wanted to reach the purest abstraction and 'the first truly unmannered and untrammelled and unentangled, styleless, universal painting.'[70] As a result, his paintings could be objective to challenge Abstract Expressionist quest for subjectivity. They could eventually be *repeated* but not *reproduced*.[71]

Reinhardt, who defined himself as a classicist, actually recovered painting's primary components to satisfy the necessary conditions of his aesthetic project.[72] Despite their seemingly iconoclastic nature, the black paintings belong to the order of painting. Painting's power was restored thanks to the colour black and the absence of representation. Every effect arises from the paint itself and is not produced by external factors such as light. This stands as a rupture with modernity since Reinhardt produced these internal effects recovering traditional pictorial practices: undercoats, transparencies, glazes.[73] For example, the photographs of

---

[66] The allovers can be seen as the explosion of his early figures into drippings – think of the figures in *Bird Effort* (1946) from the Peggy Guggenheim Collection in Venice.
[67] Damisch, 1984, p. 152.
[68] Reinhardt quoted in Crimp, 1981, p. 75.
[69] Lebensztejn, 1988, p. 40.
[70] Reinhardt, 1992, p. 55.
[71] Damisch, 1984, p. 272.
[72] On Reinhardt's classicism, see Lebensztejn, 1988, p. 40.
[73] Damisch, 'Attention: fragile: Ad Reinhardt' in Damisch, 2016, p. 135.

Ad Reinhardt in his studio as well as the details of his black paintings show that the rectangular vertical and horizontal black strips were conventionally painted, one after the other onto the painting's ground, like the draperies painted by Poussin (think of *The Adoration of the Golden Calf* from the National Gallery), whom Reinhardt placed at the origin of American Art in a cartoon titled 'How to Look at Modern Art in America' and published in *Art News* in 1961.

What to paint after Ad Reinhardt and Abstract Expressionism? Painting has repeatedly mimed its end throughout the first half of the twentieth century. What if, for once, painting mimed its Renaissance, or, the lyric memory of its own history? *The last word must always secretly be the first.*

A NEW SPIRIT IN PAINTING, 1981

II

A New History Painting: An Exhibition in the Exhibition

Je ne suis point de ceux qui en chantant
prennent toujours le même ton, et je sais
varier le mien quand je veux.
—Nicolas Poussin[74]

Io sono una sforza del passato.
Solo nella tradizione è il mio amore.
[...]
E io, feto adulto, mi aggiro
più moderno di ogni moderno
a cercare fratelli che non sono più.
—Pier Paolo Pasolini[75]

In 1981, Balthus's *Nude in Profile* (Figure 6) was hung on the most prestigious wall of the Royal Academy, on the occasion of 'A New Spirit in Painting'.[76] This work can thus be regarded as programmatic for the exhibition, since the French artist employed a technique from the Renaissance named *casearti* (a mixture of casein, gesso, plaster and oil paint, originally used to cover wood panels).[77] He learned this technique from the conservators of the Villa Medici, where he was Director from 1961 to 1976.

---

[74] Letter to Paul Fréart de Chantelou, dated from March 24, 1647. Poussin, 1824, p. 258.
[75] Pasolini, 1964, p. 26.
[76] I am indebted to Nicholas Savage, former Director of Collections at the Royal Academy of Arts, and Mark Pomeroy, Archivist at the Royal Academy of Arts, who pointed out this information to me.
[77] Balthus quoted in Roy, 1996, pp. 179-180.

His use of *casearti* was however original. *Nude in Profile* depicts the collapse of illusionism and painting's depth, in the same manner as, say, *L'Été* (1917) by Pierre Bonnard, who was Balthus's first master. Yet, Balthus's work is not embedded in the practice of "sketchlike" painting manner (*la manière esquissée*), which was part of a modernist project instigated in the eighteenth century by painters such as Hubert Robert.[78] On the contrary, Balthus made a work demanding from a technical point of view. He thus produced a double bind pairing a skilful métier with anti-illusionism (instead of illusionism) and vice versa. The canvas' topology is defined by the conjunction of two contradictory elements, which conveys an accidental meeting between two periods of (art) history. This encounter bridges what-has-been (not the past) with the now (not the present). It echoes, mutatis mutandis, Marcel Proust's description of the columns of San Marco and San Teodoro, in Piazzetta San Marco, Venice. These two columns 'keep on prolonging in our midst their days of the twelfth century, which they interpose in our today.'[79] But Balthus's aesthetic is not based on the use of artefacts dating back to past times. The entities which partly form the basis of his art are not simulacra (as described by Jean Baudrillard) either. They are rather hints of the past or memories from "Great Art". For example, the man carrying a wooden board in *La Rue* (1933) quotes Piero della Francesca's *Burial of the Wood* (one of the frescoes in the Bacci Chapel, in Arezzo), the woman lying down in *La Montagne* (1937) quotes Poussin's *Écho et Narcisse*, the woman on a ladder in *Le Cerisier* (1940) quotes Poussin's *L'Automne*. Erudite fragments incorporate new meanings. They are mingled with and inscribed into a pictorial environment to which they are arbitrarily related. This aesthetic of the hint traverses Balthus's oeuvre as well as the history of modern art. Balthus was therefore the mediator to a younger generation of a practice which had increased with the emergence of modernism. A typical example might be Picasso's *Femme à l'éventail* (1905), which echoes the Archangel

[78] Faroult in *Hubert Robert* (exh. cat.), 2016, p. 25.
[79] Proust, 1989, p. 128

Gabriel's gestures in Poussin's *Annunciation* from the National Gallery. But we can actually go back to Watteau's *Pierrot*, in which the donkey depicted in the background hints the flight into Egypt.

Such pictorial proposals are indeed generative to reassess the exhibition today. But we need an American counterpoint to Balthus's European perspective. Robert Ryman's quintessential modernist paintings might indeed be complementary to Balthus's engagement with European literary and pictorial tradition, should we like to reconfigure the narrative of the "return" to painting, combining exemplary works from 'A New Spirit in Painting' which formed an original constellation then that is still vibrant now.

Five works by Robert Ryman, all painted in 1980, were displayed in the galleries of the Royal Academy. Ryman's paintings exhibit their structure since they are procedural documents, as Naomi Spector put it.[80] *Unit* (Figure 7), *Bridge*, *Division*, *Acme* and *Crest*, can be seen as a series of paintings based on the modulation of the brushstrokes' size, the white pigment's tonal qualities, the paint's transparency and the paint's thickness. These elements were investigated for their ability to structure the composition, which Ryman wanted to reduce to the 'little simple things', in order to erase arbitrariness.[81] He also explored the figure-ground relationship through the contrasting effects triggered by the unpainted surfaces in each canvas' corners. In a Simondonian way, the works make visible and stage their making, their openness, rather than their closure.[82]

The reduction of arbitrariness thanks to the old compositional devices demands the execution of a meticulous *métier* (in a similar vein to Ad Reinhardt).[83] Ryman might thus be regarded as the last modern painter or the last modernist painter, as Yve-Alain Bois puts it.[84] This is one reason why after

---

[80] Bois, 1981, p. 93.
[81] Bois, 2009, p. 241.
[82] See Simondon, 2016, p. 247: 'It is work that must be known as a phase of technicity, not technicity as a phase of work, for it is technicity that is the whole of which work forms a part, and not the reverse.'
[83] Bois, 2009, pp. 241, 242.

Ryman and modernism, one of the solutions for painting was the "return" to figures, insofar as the (American) modernist discourse could not be maintained.

Returning to figurative painting thus signified going forward by going backward, not *contra* Ryman and modernism, but *from* and *with* Ryman and modernism. Younger painters could look at Ryman's works like an outstanding alphabet of forms, materials and brushstrokes. Traditions and recognisable motifs were indeed recovered but researches on painting's formal structures were however not abandoned. The painters who "returned" to figuration renewed ties with painting as a mode of knowledge and thus critically displaced Conceptual art. By and large, they reconciled a form of painting at the service of the mind, to speak like Duchamp, with a form of painting that invests fully the visual level. Each of their works is a dynamic struggle between an idea and a picture.

NEO-EXPRESSIONISTS?

Schwarz-Rot-Gold dythirambisch I (Figure 1) *II & III* is a triptych that belongs to the series Lüpertz inaugurated in 1963: *dithyrambisch malerei.* Dithyramb refers to poetry honouring the God Dionysius in Antique Greece, perhaps best exemplified in Timotheus of Miletus's works. The resonances between the sounds form the basis of dithyrambic poems, in which grammar is often jeopardised for the benefit of tonal qualities.[85] Similarly, in Lüpertz's paintings, the

[84] Bois, 1981, p. 103 and Bois, 2009, p. 241. Robert Storr might have misunderstood this statement originally coined in French. He claimed, against Bois, that 'Ryman has explicitly rejected the idea that we are witnessing the finale of modernism.' First, Strorr's counterexample was a quotation by Ryman which does not mention modernism but abstraction. Second, in French, 'the last' does not necessarily mean 'the ultimate' or 'the finale', but implies that the subject referred to as 'the last' incorporated the objective characteristics of the idea he or she investigated. This is one reason why Bois acknowledged that for Ryman painting is in its infancy, and mentioned Ryman's irony about the death of painting. See Storr, *Robert Ryman* (exh. cat.), 1993, pp. 39, 45.

[85] See Kneubühler in *Lüpertz* (exh. cat.), 1993, p. 24 and Lukinovitch in *Lüpertz* (exh. cat.), 1993, pp. 30-31.

correspondences between forms and colours are greater than their referential character, that is why the title only refers to colours. The rhymes between the figures, to speak like a French academician from the eighteenth century, follow, in the first instance, a logic of sensation (as described by Gilles Deleuze) since their effects are physical and physiological.

To make a comparison with music, the figures are like the *libretti* written by Lorenzo Da Ponte for Mozart's trilogy, insofar as the power of Da Ponte's *libretti* lies in their ability to be in harmony with Mozart's compositions (think of the duetto Fiordiligi-Dorabella opening the second scene of the first act in *Cosí fan tutte*).[86] This is exactly what appealed to Diderot in Italian opera. He 'applaud[ed] [...] the victory of expressive intonation over discourse, the latter's deconstruction carried out for the benefit of musical requirements.'[87]

In *Schwarz-Rot-Gold,* the most subtle variations within the composition might be the contrasts between the blue *field*[88] and the unpainted surface in the top right-hand corner of each panel: effects of rhythm are produced by the modulation of the size of each blue field and each unpainted surface. These effects are also enhanced by the large format of the panels, which is not an argument from authority but rather a means to intensify the triptych's visuality.

Lüpertz's own interpretation of dithyrambic poetry is a transformation (*Umgestaltung*) in Aby Warburg's sense of the word. In his essay on Manet's *Déjeuner sur l'herbe,* Warburg wrote that 'great works are those which do not borrow their force of penetration (*ihre Durchschlagskraft*) from a setting-aside (*Beseitigung*) of old forms but from their transformation (*Umgestaltung*).'[89] Beyond the explicit reference to a source from Classical Antiquity, Lüpertz displaced

[86] 'Io sono felice! / Se questo mio core / Mai cangia desio, / Amore mi faccia / Vivendo penar.' ("Ah guarda sorella", I, 2)
[87] Lyotard, 2011, pp. 209-210.
[88] I am here borrowing the translation of the French word *aplat* from the translation of Deleuze's *Bacon* by Daniel W. Smith – assuming that it is not related to colour field painting.
[89] Warburg quoted in Damisch, 1996, p. 218. Damisch's interpretation of Warburg's transformation was also embedded in Lévi-Strauss' transformation; see Lévi-Strauss, 2008, p. 978.

dithyrambic poetry from the textual to the pictorial, and from Antiquity to the twentieth century. In other words, he transformed a linguistic model producing poetic sounds into a formalist model producing a chromatic logic of sensation. Lüpertz's operation is structural and historical. He thus reconfigured (as is implied by *Umgestaltung*) an artistic artefact from the past in order to expand its meaning in the now.

Lüpertz was also drawn to the work of Francis Bacon. He wanted 'to avoid the figurative, illustrative, and narrative character [of the] Figure', which he isolated to 'break with representation.'[90] As such, the figures he depicted are a matter of sensation, as in the upper half of El Greco's *The Burial of the Count of Orgaz*.[91] Lüpertz erased the referential character of his German motifs to establish a free play of colours and painterly elements. Modernism was therefore acknowledged since representation was overcome.

The comparison between Bacon and Lüpertz may be explored further through one of Bacon's paintings included in 'A New Spirit in Painting'. For example, *Landscape* (Figure 8), one of the late paintings Bacon made, both essentialising and intensifying his early works. The *diagrammatic*[92] nature of the *grassy motif*[93] allows for the erasure of its referential character. Its pictorial power is enhanced by its relationships and resonances with the other figures forming the composition.[94] The most eloquent compositional elements might be the two red arrows, which are, actually, two Euclidean vectors, in the sense that they would be used in physics to model forces. What forces?

In *Landscape*, the two vectors seem to be a post-Cezannian

---

[90] Deleuze, 2003, p. 2. For the original version, see Deleuze, 2002, p. 12.
[91] Deleuze, 2002, p. 18. Deleuze, 2003, p. 9.
[92] For a definition of the diagram see Deleuze, 2002, pp. 95-96 and Deleuze, 2003, pp. 101-102: [...] the operative set of asignifying and nonrepresentative lines and zones, line- strokes and colorpatches. [...] the operation of the diagram, its function, says Bacon, is to be "suggestive." [...] The diagram is [...] a chaos, a catastrophe, but it is also a germ of order or rhythm. It is a violent chaos in relation to the figurative givens, but it is a germ of rhythm in relation to the new order of the painting. As Bacon says, it "unlocks areas of sensation".'
[93] Leiris, 2008, p. 26.
[94] See Deleuze, 2002, p. 65.

device. They embody the pictorial forces which trigger the movements (*Bewegungen*) within the composition. Cézanne transposed the wind's directions in his paintings, equating the nature of his brushstrokes with the ways the wind blew to embrace the landscape. One could think of the foliage in *Château noir* (Figure 9): branches' geometry is undermined by the leaves' tones of green, which sparkle and envelop the dark scenery. The superimposed brushstrokes go back and forth, our gaze penetrates the landscape's vibrations as the painting breathes. After Damisch's clouds, maybe shall we consider the wind as a theoretical object that foregrounds the whole history of painting? The point of departure, or, arrival, would be the three Nereids from the Nereid Monument, now in the British Museum.[95] In Cézanne's paintings, the vectors *are* the brushstrokes. Bacon took a step forward hypostasising with simple symbols the movements at work within the composition. The two red vectors signal where the *pictorial wind* comes from. The directions of the red vectors (from the top left-hand corner to the bottom right-hand corner and vice versa) correspond to the directions of the curvy lines forming the grassy motif. The network of relationships between the vectors and the diagram is a matrix of sensations which subordinates forms to colours.

Similarly, Anselm Kiefer investigated representation displacing another set of classical compositional devices: the frame, the ground and the picture plane.[96] In *Bilderstreit* (from the Van Abbemuseum, Eindhoven), the central motif is a palette – a motif Kiefer repeatedly used to tackle representation insofar as the palette is the attribute of painters in classical art. *Bilderstreit* belongs, moreover, to an eponymous series Kiefer started in 1978.[97] In this regard, the names that encircle the palette refer to the debate between the iconodules and the iconoclasts, crystallised by the first and

[95] The *Ninfa,* as described by Warburg in his essay on Botticelli, might be the most canonical example of this paradigm. This feminine figure from Antiquity appears, for example, in Botticelli's *Primavera* and Ghirlandaio's *Natività della Vergine.* On Aby Warburg's interest in the wind as a figure in Quattrocento painting, see Didi-Huberman, 2003.

[96] Arasse, 2001, p. 300.

[97] *Ibid.*, pp. 98, 99, 105. On Kiefer's palettes, see the chapter 'Palettes', pp. 97-113.

the second iconoclastic controversies, which took place in the Byzantine Empire under Leo III and Leo V. This reference is also conveyed by the colour symbolism: the iconodules' names (Theodora, Eirene...) are written in white while the iconoclasts' names (Leo III, Leo V...) are written in black. *Bilderstreit* has mistakenly been interpreted as a post-Auschwitz work.[98] Indeed, its central meaning lies elsewhere: Kiefer's take on the iconoclastic controversy actually depicts iconoclasm as the principle of artistic creation, the necessary condition to resurrect images.[99]

The palette frames the dark landscape depicted.[100] If *Bilderstreit* was a classical painting, one would say that the surface enframed by the palette is the space of presentation, within the representation. The palette's parerga are not only the Byzantine names but also the tanks. The drips of red paint and the red cuts show that the palette is wounded. For if the dialectical relationship between the ergon and the parergon is conveyed by the contrast between the lake's stasis (an empty space) and the figures' movements in Poussin's *Pyrame et Thisbé* (Figure 3), it is conveyed by the tanks' attacks on the palette in Kiefer's *Bilderstreit*. The tanks hollow out the palette and consequently jeopardise the figure-ground relationship.

The parergon in *Bilderstreit* could therefore be understood from the definition given by Jacques Derrida in *The Truth in Painting*, against Kant (for whom the parergon introduces the ergon). For Derrida, the parergon distorts the ergon and points out the lack inherent in the very thing it frames.[101] Anselm Kiefer, as for him, might have depicted the

---

[98] See, for example, Rosenthal, M. in *Anselm Kiefer* (exh. cat.), 1987, p. 79.
[99] See Anselm Kiefer in conversation with Götz Adriani in *The Early Years of the Old Masters: Baselitz - Richter - Polke - Kiefer* (exh. cat.), p. 284: 'The iconoclastic controversy interested me very early on, and I've not only painted pictures on the subject, I've also taken photos of toy tanks in the attic in Hornbach shooting a palette to pieces. Iconoclasm has two sides for me. On the one hand [...] it refers to the fleeting nature of artistic fame, or fame in general. On the other hand, iconoclasm for me is the principle of artistic creation, because without the destruction of images there is no way to find new ones, no resurrection of the image. One image always erases another; it's a process of constant self-abolition and rebirth.'
[100] Arasse, 2001, p. 100.
[101] Derrida, 1978, pp. 49, 73, 83, 92-94. See the chapter 'Parergon', (pp. 44-94)

nature of painting in 1977: the centre of his work is destroyed and the palette only frames a thick layer of paint. This very layer of paint actually proves to be a *pentimento*, as is shown by the painting's upper corners, whose soft colours hint the original presence of a landscape. The dialectical relationship between the abandoned composition and the wounded palette symbolises failure as much as Kiefer's understanding of the stakes of the iconoclastic controversy.

Kiefer sought to undermine painting dismantling the frame, the ground and the picture plane. In other words, the 'presentational devices which [...] constitute the general framework of representation'[102] – that is to say, 'the devices which ensure the coherence and autonomy of classical painting.'[103] *Bilderstreit* shows that "Great Art" might now be going towards the presentation of the 'trace' of the Idea, the depiction of its ruins, that is why Kiefer considers the palette as a 'symbol for an idea, [...] a sign for something spiritual.'[104] These strategies are intensified by the materiality of the painting: the powerful brushstrokes show the marks left by the painter on the canvas, as if the painting was the memory of the artist's body, which is depicted in the lower half of the composition.[105]

PHILIP GUSTON AND CY TWOMBLY: AMERICANS AGAINST THE GRAIN

The works of Lüpertz and Kiefer have unveiled that they are neither postmodern nor a mere meditation on the aftermath of the Second World War.[106] The common

---

in which Derrida exemplifies his argument inserting blank spaces into the body of the text, to produce a "framework effect". The difference between Derrida and Marin is that, for the former, the parergon does not produce any image while, for the latter, the parergon produces an image. For Marin, the *representation* of the king is the *presentation* of the king. See for example Marin, *Le Portait du roi*, 1981, pp. 35-36.

[102] Marin quoted in Arasse, 2001, p. 300.

[103] Arasse, 2001, p. 300.

[104] *Ibid.*, pp. 303, 306 and note 27 above. See also Anselm Kiefer in conversation with Richard Calvocoressi in Anselm Kiefer *Uraeus* (exh. cat.), 2019, p. 18.

[105] On Kiefer's exploration of the body as a painterly element see Arasse, 2001, p. 67.

ground between the so-called Neo-Expressionists and older painters from 'A New Spirit in Painting' also invalidates the postmodern critique. I would now like to take a look at Philip Guston's *Door* (Figure 10) and Cy Twombly's *Bacchanalia*.

Guston's painting depicts a door. This door is not right-side up. Guston rotated the figure ninety degrees. He chose 'to maintain the figure-ground relation in ambiguity, in permanent indecision. If it is true that form is not reducible to the geometrical outline of objects but rather remains connected with the texture of things and appeals simultaneously to all our senses, [Guston] has returned to the notion of form its original meaning by treating figures as vaguely silhouetted grounds.'[107] Guston thus used that motif as a compositional tool to interrogate painting's ability to represent objects.

But further ambiguities are at work in the painting. First, Guston blurred the elements in the black field, as if he had painted vanishing objects. The main ambiguity lies, however, in the door itself. One cannot determine if one half of the door is hidden by the red field, or, if Guston simply painted half a door. This door cannot be opened and is characterised by its iconographical and iconological density. In 1965, Guston was drawn to one painting from the Renaissance depicting a door: Piero della Francesca's *Flagellazione* (Figure 11). As Guston put it, 'we can move spatially everywhere, as in life' in Piero's painting since 'the architectural box is opened by the large block of the discoursers to the right, as if a door were slid aside to reveal its contents.'[108] The possibility of moving

---

[106] For a postmodern critique of German Neo-Expressionists, see Foster, 1985, pp. 44-48 (in 1985, Foster did not see anything in their works but pluralism, subjectivism, primitivism, and thus a failed repetition of Expressionism through a capitalist celebration of the irrational) and Buchloh, 1981, pp. 55, 61-62. For the historiographical significance of Deleuze's *Bacon*, see Darragon, *The Michael Werner Collection* (exh. cat.), 2012, pp 28-29: 'It is a book in movement that isolates the monad Bacon from his London setting, as Foucault specified the exemplary quality of an abstract Velázquez.' For the historiographical significance of Arasse's *Kiefer*, see Cohn, 2010, pp. 257-270 and Cohn, 2009, p. 118: 'Kiefer's oeuvre was classicised, degermanised and decontextualised from its links with nazism by Daniel Arasse's interpretation.' (my trans.)

[107] I borrowed this formulation from Hubert Damisch's analysis of Jean Dubuffet's oeuvre. He derived it from Maurice Merleau-Ponty's *Phenomenology of Perception*. See Damisch, 2014, p. 313 and note 33, p. 316.

[108] Guston, 2011, p. 41.

spatially in paintings, as in life, is precisely, what has been lost after modernity. Guston's scene is all the more impermeable as it is made of impastos and thick brushstrokes. It seems that Guston closed the door in Piero's work to paint what saddens the contemporary eye: the disappearance of painting's space and illusion.

Guston, after returning to figuration in 1969, reflected on painting transforming and reconfiguring pictorial references from the past, like Lüpertz and Kiefer.[109] He thus investigated painting depicting objects from which a myriad of images can emerge as they refer both to the history of painting and to the painter's studio – think of *Ladder* (1978) from the NGA or *Table and Stretchers* (1978) from the Yale University Art Gallery. Such references can be found in some of Robert Rauschenberg's works, which explore those objects in three dimensions – take, for example, *Pink Door* (1954) or the ladders from *Winter Pool* (1959) and *The Frightened Gods of Fortune* (1981). American artists' renewed interest in the history of European painting also found echoes across the career of Cy Twombly, who had moved to Rome in 1957.[110]

Four drawings by Twombly on the theme of the Bacchanalia, all achieved in 1977, were included in 'A New Spirit in Painting'. They are focused on Bacchic rites celebrating death and rebirth. Twombly made them after seeing a Poussin exhibition held at the Villa Medici in honour of Balthus. Twombly's drawings are actually transformations of Poussin's drawings: *Fall (Five Days in October)* transformed *Armida Bearing the Sleeping Rinaldo*; *Fall (Five Days in November)* transformed *The Triumph of Pan*; *Winter (Five Days in January)* transformed *Venus at the Fountain*; *Winter (Five Days in February)* transformed *Extreme Unction*. The drawings Twombly collaged had been extracted from *L'Univers de Poussin*, a monograph published in 1977 and devoted to the French painter's drawings.[111]

---

[109] Slifkin, 2013, pp. 22, 26-28.
[110] On Guston's engagement with the history of painting, see Rishel in *Philip Guston* (exh. cat.), 2003.
[111] Schmidt in *Twombly and Poussin* (exh. cat.), 2011, p. 78 and *Twombly and Poussin* (exh. cat.), pp. 140-147.

The chains of transformation specific to Twombly's drawings are actually longer than the mere relationship between Poussin and Twombly. Indeed, *Armida Bearing the Sleeping Rinaldo* is based on Torquato Tasso's *La Gerusalemme Liberata*; *The Triumph of Pan* stems from a vase by Salpion of Athens depicting the birth of Bacchus; *Venus at the Fountain* is the illustration of the description of the Fountain of Love in Philostratus' *Imagines*.

We can go back to Classical Antiquity from Twombly: he was Poussin's contemporary as much as Poussin was a contemporary of the classical poets and artists whose works he transformed.[112] Twombly steps before us with the guiding torch, and we shall follow.[113] Yet, how did Twombly transform Poussin's drawings? Can we establish that Twombly's drawings are transformations in their own right? How is the transformation achieved from a formal point of view?

Twombly veiled (think of *Five Days in November*) or drew on (think of *Five Days in October, January*, and *February*) the reproductions of Poussin's drawings. Blurring these images might have been a strategy to signify their travel through time. However, what is really at stake in these quotations? As Hubert Damisch suggested, the drawing reproductions do not function like cubist collages since their effects are not uncanny. On the contrary, they double Twombly's drawings and function like a framework, establishing a frontier – or, to speak like Louis Marin, a *lisière*[114] – between themselves and their surroundings, the parerga Twombly depicted, or, maybe shall we paradoxically say: the ergon Twombly depicted around the parergon.[115] Either way, what did Twombly depict around Poussin's drawings?

Each painting bears its title. Twombly transcribed the memory of a culture which is gone and whose sole surviving trace would be words.[116] The titles are reminiscences per se,

---

[112] Damisch, 1996, p. 199.

[113] See Warburg quoted in Gombrich, 1986, p. 273: 'Manet steps before me with the guiding torch, and I shall follow. (*Manet tritt mit der Fürherfackel vor mich hin, und ich werde folgen*)'

[114] Marin, 1993, pp. 410-411.

[115] Damisch, 'Quant au titre. Cy Twombly' in Damisch, 2016, p. 45.

[116] See Barthes, 'Cy Twombly ou *Non multa sed multum*', in Barthes, 1982, pp. 147.

as if the word 'bacchanalia' encapsulated the history of the ancient Mediterranean world. 'Bacchanalia' thus functions like the name 'Guermantes', as understood by the Narrator in *La Recherche*.[117] Moreover, Twombly's Dionysian handwriting undermines the Apollonian classical references and conveys the ecstasy of ancient Bacchic rites. But colours are perhaps more Dionysian than Twombly's gestures.

For Barthes, Twombly is a colourist inasmuch as his colours are *materia prima*, as described by the alchemists.[118] Rather, I would like to suggest that Twombly's colours are what Lodovico Dolce called *colorito* (colouring) as opposed to *colore* (colour).[119] For Dolce, the *colorito* is painting's element *par excellence*. It is the thoughtful application of colours which does not rely on the colours' primary qualities.[120] In Twombly's works included in 'A New Spirit in Painting', we can see neither the colours he used nor a colour that is prominent. The coloured surfaces stand alone. They are a condensate of colours. Twombly's powerful strokes, sometimes blurred or erased, heighten the surfaces' physicality. These very surfaces are organically linked to Poussin's drawings. They translate into colours the Bacchic rites' essence, as if they were the substrate or the survivals (*Nachleben*) of the sources they stem from.

Guston's and Twombly's strategies reveal in an exemplary way the common ground between their works and Neo-Expressionist paintings. But another painter perhaps epitomises the *new spirit in painting*.

BASELITZ AT THE CROSSROADS

Baselitz's *Fingermalerei-Adler* (Figure 12) is the epitome of what was perceived as a regression in the 1980s. The eagle

---

[117] Proust, Vol. 3, 1992, p. 12: '*le nom de Guermantes d'alors est aussi comme un de ces petits ballons dans lesquels on a enfermé de l'oxygène ou un autre gaz*'.

[118] Barthes, 'Cy Twombly ou *Non multa sed multum*', in Barthes, 1982, p. 153 and Barthes, 'Sagesse de l'art' in Barthes, 1982, p. 163.

[119] Dolce, 1557, p. 164.

[120] *Ibid.*, pp. 184-185: '*Né creda alcuno che la forza del colorito consista nella scelta de' bei colori, come belle lache, bei azzurri, bei verdi e simili; percioché questi colori sono belli parimente senza che e' si mettano in opera.*'

commonly symbolises the old Germany and individual freedom.[121] However, understanding Baselitz's eagle as the assertion of his own individuality as well as a light and ahistorical quotation of German iconography would be reductive. What is really at stake in this painting?

Although Baselitz had already started composing his paintings upside down in 1972, we cannot help thinking that we are witnessing the eagle's fall, which exhibits painting's *gravity*[122] and might investigate the Christian motif of the Fall of Man. The eagle also conjures up the tradition of still life and the motif of poultry hanging – think of Chardin's *Still Life with Dead Pheasant* (Figure 13). This hypothesis echoes Baselitz's engagement with Chaïm Soutine's oeuvre, which he discovered in 1959 after seeing Soutine's *Boeuf écorché*, a painting based on a 1655 work by Rembrandt now in the Louvre.[123] This influence might also lie in Soutine's works depicting dead birds after Chardin (Figure 14). Moreover, the falling feather at the top left-hand corner symbolises the artist's tools. As a natural element, it reinforces the painting's organicity, which is also highlighted by the title: *Fingermalerei*. But the feather can symbolise death as well – think of the details in Pieter Brueghel's *Landscape with the Fall of Icarus*.[124] One could also think of the Ganymede myth as well as the ways it has been depicted over the centuries – take, for example, Rubens's *Abduction of Ganymede* (Figure 15). Baselitz's eagle could thus be seen as a metamorphosis of Zeus desperately looking for Ganymede and chasing beauty – we could imagine

---

[121] On the eagle's symbolism see Waldman, in *Georg Baselitz* (exh. cat), 1995, pp. 73-75. See also Meuli, 1987 for an analysis of the eagle as a conceptual motif and strategy in Baselitz's oeuvre. Interestingly, Marcel Broodthaers, who was acquainted with Baselitz through Michael Werner (who offered Broodthaers to be included in 'A New Spirit in Painting'), explored at the same time the motif of the eagle in his 'Musée d'Art Moderne, Département des Aigles' (1968-1972) to criticise Conceptual artists' claims about the 'the disappearance of the iconographic, the elimination of the visual, and the transcendance of all historical structures imposed by the classificatory systems of the museums' (Buchloh, 2004, p. 552). For an account of Broodthaers's 'Musée d'Art Moderne, Département des Aigles', see Buchloh, 2004.

[122] On the notion of gravity in painting, see Étienne Jollet's analysis of Fragonard's *Perrette* (Jollet, 1993).

[123] Waldman, in *Georg Baselitz* (exh. cat), 1995, p. 17.

[124] Didi-Huberman, 1989, pp. 140-142.

Baselitz wandering through the Garden of Ganymede in the Boboli Gardens, during his 1965 stay at the Villa Romana in Florence.

However, the motif of the eagle retrospectively echoes a twelfth-century *Physiologus* from the library of the Evangelical School of Smyrna (Figure 16), which Baselitz investigated in *Malelade*.[125] The *Physiologus* is a medieval natural history aimed at unifying texts and images to illustrate the creation of the animals.[126] According to the *Physiologus* (the description of which is derived from the Psalm 103:5), the eagle became blind and its wings heavier as it grew old. The eagle's youth was then renewed after it flew to the sun to burn its old wings and after it plunged into a spring.[127] This narrative resonates with Greek myths such as the Fountain of Youth and the myth of Daedalus and Icarus. It thus stages a dialectical relationship between death and rebirth (also conveyed by Twombly's *Bacchanalia* or Kiefer's *Bilderstreit*), which might be a paradigmatic metaphor of painting in the twentieth century: repeatedly sentenced to death but still alive.

Another essential element to the meaning of *Adler* is the use of Willem de Kooning's brushstrokes. De Kooning's works are primarily the nostalgic enlarged depiction of bodies' flesh from Renaissance painting. But they are also the expansion of Soutine's Céret paintings, which de Kooning saw at the Barnes and which are characterised by energetic brush marks and the intertwinement of serpentine lines – take, for example, *Groupe d'arbres* (Figure 17), another wind-blown landscape.[128] *Untitled II* (Figure 18) illustrates de Kooning's strategy and was hung in front of Baselitz's *Adler* on the occasion of 'A New Spirit in Painting'. Nonetheless, Baselitz's brushstrokes are not strictly the reproduction of de Kooning's brushstrokes. Indeed, the German painter diminished the

[125] Baselitz in conversation with the author, January 18, 2018, Fondation Beyeler, Riehen/Basel.
[126] Strzygowski, 1899, pp. 103, and Bernabó, 1998, pp. 5, 12.
[127] Strzygowski, 1899, p. 19.
[128] Sylvester in *Willem de Kooning* (exh. cat.), 1994, pp. 22-23, 25. Similarly, Louis Marin established a link between de Kooning and Dutch and Flemish painting, imagining a fictive dialogue across time between the Dutch-American artist's paintings and Rubens's, Rembrandt's, Vermeer's, Jan van Goyen's as well as

size of the Dutch painter's brushstrokes, he displaced and transformed them, as is shown by the details (Figure 19).

Baselitz named his method '*passatismo*' as opposed to futurism.[129] *Adler* shows the intertwinement of two fragments of time, staging a clash between the Middle Ages and the twentieth century. It is moreover crucial to notice that any transformation results from the painter's rigorous and total engagement with a given source, not from the mere quotation of a style or an image. Baselitz actually combined two chains of transformation: on the one hand, Rembrandt-Soutine-de Kooning-Baselitz, on the other, *Physiologus*-Baselitz. In this respect, the meaning of the artwork rather lies in Baselitz's interpretation of his sources rather than in the meaning of the sources themselves. The encounter between what-has-been and the now allows for the emergence of something new. Baselitz therefore composed with the same force of Mozart, whom combined baroque fugues and classical phrases in his 41st symphony (think of the second movement).

A NEW HISTORY PAINTING?

The montage of several works from 'A New Spirit in Painting' allows for the establishment of a taxonomy categorising the main principles characteristic of the *new spirit in painting*. Five strategies have been identified above:

Hercules Seghers's works. For Louis Marin, de Kooning (who described himself as an 'eclectic painter by chance') could be the example of what the "real" history of *modern art* might be: a logic driven by chance, which expresses itself through the totality of the forms and styles historically available and possible. This indeterministic logic might be an alternative to a critical evaluation of modern and contemporary art's trajectory underpinned by the notion of *crisis*, as criticised by Marin. Looking at de Kooning's painting, the viewer's task is thus the search and the acknowledgement of the Dutch *smile* or the Flemish *smile*. As de Kooning put it, 'if I am influenced by a painter from another time, that's like the smile of the Cheshire Cat in *Alice*; the smile left over when the cat is gone. In other words, I could be influenced by Rubens, but I would certainly not paint like Rubens.' See Marin in *Willem de Kooning* (exh. cat.), 1984, pp. 31-32, 33, 39.

[129] Baselitz in conversation with the author, January 18, 2018, Fondation Beyeler, Riehen/Basel. The notion of '*passatismo*' was used by Filippo Tommaso Marinetti as an opposite to futurism.

the transformation of an ancient textual source into a structure for painting (Lüpertz); the transformation of classical painting's structure (Kiefer); the reflection on painting embedded in pictorial issues raised by early modern and Renaissance paintings (Guston); the direct transformation of works of the past (Twombly); the artwork as a time-machine, that goes from century to century, lets us see through the artist's eyes and travel through the world he built (Baselitz).

The painters we have looked at were not striving for the conservation of figuration in the 1970s. Their paintings are not strictly figurative or representational. They are rather the place of a dialectic tension and a dynamic balance between abstraction and figuration. They convey a paradox which might have foregrounded the whole history of painting as is shown by Giotto's *Capella degli Scrovegni*, in which one can either follow the logic of the *storia* or be enveloped by the paint as Daniel Arasse put it.[130] The paradox is also temporal and historical. More than being an act of dandyism and the egocentric exhibition of a sophisticated visual literacy, these paintings bridge what-has-been and the now. They are, nonetheless, neither variations on past paintings nor contemporary compositions merely enlivened with old, yet fashionable, accessories. They might be a new kind of history painting. They are however not to be understood as the representation of mythologised historical events. They are at most the representation of the history of painting itself, or, the representation of history, understood here as 'the lyric resurrection of past bodies' as Roland Barthes put it.[131] These paintings demonstrate that the forces of freedom of arts depend neither on the artist's political and public engagement, nor in the doctrinal, sometimes journalistic, content of the artwork. Arts' forces of freedom lie in the displacement of the established language and forms as Roland Barthes has showed, *contra* Sartre, in his lecture in inauguration of the Chair of Literary Semiology at the Collège de France.[132]

---

[130] Arasse, 2003.
[131] Barthes, 1979, p. 15. For the original version see 1978, p. 43.
[132] Barthes, 1978, p. 17; 1979, p. 6.

Balthus, Baselitz, Twombly, Guston, Kiefer and Lüpertz painted works which mirror in an original manner the history of painting, after having seen the Old Masters with fresh eyes. The same could be said about further artists from 'A New Spirit in Painting' such as Rainer Fetting – who refreshed the theme of bathers (Figure 26), A.R. Penck – whose black paintings stem from Japanese and Chinese calligraphy, Brice Marden – 'whose paintings could be called classical [...] because of the specificity of the plane'[133], Sigmar Polke – who used lapis lazuli in reference to Grünewald's *Isenheim Altarpiece*, or Gerhard Richter – take, for example, his five-part series (Figure 20), derived from Tiziano's *Annunciation* (Figure 21), which transformed light and shadows intensifying the diagonal that distributes light from the bottom left-hand corner to the top right-hand corner.

Their paintings are 'a journey which lands us in a country free by default; angels and dragons are no longer there to defend it'; where 'our gaze can fall [...] upon certain old and lovely things, whose signified is abstract [...]. It is [...] a moment of gentle apocalypse, a historical moment of the greatest possible pleasure.'[134] Pasolini did not only exemplify Barthes's lecture because he "abjured" his *Trilogy of Life*[135] but also because he displaced forms from the past into the now. For example, Pasolini used latin grammar to write in Italian in *Poesia in forma di rosa*, he quoted Fiorentino's and Pontormo's *Deposizione* in *La Ricotta* – which are not anachronic quotations since Pasolini was interested in these paintings' meaning in 1963 rather than in their meaning in the Cinquecento.

However, the interpretation of the works should not be dualist but monist, so that the form is not separated from the content and is thus related to the works' historicity. The difficulty to refer to the painters above mentioned through a concept encompassing their own practice invites us to reflect on the conceptualisation of their aesthetic attitude.

---

[133] Lebensztejn, 1988, p. 40
[134] Barthes, 1978, p. 41; 1979, p. 14.
[135] Barthes, 1978, p. 27; 1979, p. 9.

THE ANTIMODERNS

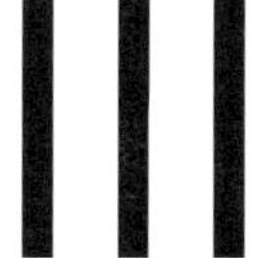

The Emergence of the Antimodern

> *Je me rendais compte que le temps qui passe n'amène pas forcément le progrès dans les arts. […] [T]el auteur du XVIIe siècle, qui n'a connu ni la Révolution française, ni les découvertes scientifiques, ni la guerre, peut être supérieur à tel écrivain d'aujourd'hui […].*
>
> —Marcel Proust[136]

For Marxist critics, Neo-Expressionism was a form of postmodernism. It was said to be an alienation from history because of its eclecticism and its lack of historicism.[137] Rosalind Krauss, for whom history is a progressive notion, suggested that Neo-Expressionism was an antimodernist postmodernism, as opposed to a critical postmodernism, led by the Pictures generation, which emerged in the 1970s.[138] But the postmodern critics of the 1970s and the 1980s instrumentalised the so-called Pictures generation artists (Cindy Sherman, Sherrie Levine, Gretchen Bender and so on). They saw in these artists the manifestation of the *neo-avant-garde*[139] and the theories they advocated. They consequently praised what they thought to be the artists' concerns with contemporary political events – such

136 Proust, Vol. 7, 1992, p. 290.
137 Buchloh, 1981, p. 54 and Foster, 1985, p. 44.
138 Krauss, 2016, p. 675.
139 For a definition of neo-avant-garde, see Buchloh, 2000, p. 356.

a reading has however been deconstructed by Arasse's analysis of Cindy Sherman's *Untitled photographs.*[140] Hal Foster established a distinction, similar to the one of Krauss, between a neoconservative and a poststructuralist postmodernism.[141] For the postmodern critique, the Neo-Expressionists are antimodernist in their apparent attempt to preclude modernism by recovering old cultural traditions. Such a strategy was said to be the product of neoliberalism and the pastiche of the values promoted by Neo-Expressionism.[142] However the postmodern critics forgot the forces of freedom of arts described by Barthes.

In no instance is painting in thrall to a linear and progressive historical time. The artists are free to wander back in time and space to revisit art history and their own oeuvre, disregarding the idea of progress. The best example is Picasso who absorbed history to develop his own logic. His late works shown in the central hall of the Royal Academy provided young painters with an outstanding example of what painting can be, as Baselitz (who has described his own oeuvre as a cosmos) later recalled.[143] For example, *Child with a Spade* (Figure 22) could have been painted at almost any time in Picasso's career, insofar as Picasso combined the motif of the double-face, which he explored from the 1930s portraying Dora Maar, the motif of the musketeer, the motif of the child and so on and so forth.

The denial of Neo-Expressionism's qualities because of its apparent traditionalism echoes Gerhard Richter's characterisation of 'people [who] are always upset when confronted with something traditional and conservative.'[144] The affinities between the Neo-Expressionists and artists outside the "postmodern generation" show the necessity to conceptualise a notion that acknowledges on the one hand, the

---

140 See Arasse, 1999 and Dagen, 2009.
141 Foster, 2016, p. 699.
142 *Ibid.*, pp. 699-700; Buchloh, 1981, pp. 72-73; Habermas, 1983, p. 14., Foster, 1985, p. 127.
143 See Baselitz in conversation with the author, January 18, 2018, Fondation Beyeler, Riehen/Basel and Baselitz quoted in Ottinger in *Picasso.Mania* (exh. cat.), 2016, p. 235.
144 Richter quoted in Storr, *Gerhard Richter* (exh. cat), 2002, p. 64.

existence of a third way between 'the partisans of progress and modernity and the partisans of tradition, or of regression';[145] on the other hand, the irrelevance and inaccurracy of postmodernism, which 'is not a serious category', as T.J. Clark puts it.[146]

The Neo-Expressionists and their older fellow painters are *antimodern* – not in the sense that they radically reject modernity and want to restore a system from the past. On the contrary, they are modern with a vengeance, their ambition is not to take refuge in the past but to imagine the future the past requires us to embrace. They are the Nietzschean inactuals *par excellence*: they live contemporaneously with their ancestors, dialoguing with them across time; their works, both unhistorical and historical, are the product of the *plastic power of man* (i.e. 'the capacity [...] to transform and incorporate into oneself what is past and foreign, [...] to replace what has been lost').[147]

The notion of *antimodern* originally refers to writers such as Chateaubriand, Baudelaire, Flaubert, Proust or Barthes. It was coined by Antoine Compagnon, after Charles Du Bos and Jacques Maritain, for whom *antimodern* was the equivalent of *ultramodern*.[148] We can now displace this concept from literary theory to art history.

For Compagnon, six constants define the antimodern: the Counter-Revolution, the Anti-Enlightenment, the doctrine of original sin, the sublime, pessimism and vituperation.[149] Among these constants, the Anti-Enlightenment might be the main characteristic of antimodern painting since the former as much as the latter are embedded in realism as opposed to idealism. Antimodern realism is perhaps best exemplified in Edmund Burke's *Reflections on the Revolution in France*, which was written thirty three years after *On the Sublime and Beautiful* (1757), and thus bridged aesthetics and

[145] Lefebvre, 1983, p. 1.
[146] *Modernism and Modernity*, 1983, p. 265.
[147] Nietzsche, 1997, pp. 60, 62, 63, 95, 106, 111, 120.
[148] Compagnon, 2005, p. 8.
[149] *Ibid.*, p. 17.

political philosophy.[150] By and large, Burke's essay exemplifies the antimodern conception of historicism since it values the lessons of history over abstract concepts and considers history as a 'great volume unrolled for our instruction.'[151] However, the antimoderns did not intend to blindly conserve past objects. Rather, they made the most of these objects, transforming their very morphological structures. Antimodernity is therefore not retrograde and its aesthetic project might be epitomised in Chateaubriand's *Mémoires d'outre-tombe*:

> [...] let us look back with veneration to the past ages which are rendered sacred by the memory and the relics of our ancestors; at the same time let us not attempt to retrograde toward them, for they have no longer any thing real in common with us, and should we attempt to seize them they would vanish.[152]

The antimoderns' creative process is not based on the mere *repetition* of the past but on the *transformation* of the relics of the past. This is one reason why Chateaubriand's *Genius of Christianity* did not reflect on the restoration of the Ancien Régime but on the ways to re-introduce Christianity in France. The antimoderns faced similar issues: how to paint and go forward without forgetting the fecund energies of the past? How not to be a vulgar amanuensis?

The antimoderns transform past works to prevent themselves from repeating them. However, the transformation is nothing more than a method. Hence, the real issue is: can we conceptualise a notion that acknowledges the mnemonic function of antimodern works?

The antimoderns' material is memory: they sculpt time brushing paint on the canvas. They thus (re)mediate the past, swinging between bygone days and the now. In mathematics, their works would be translated by a

---

[150] *Ibid.*, p. 49.
[151] *Ibid.*, p. 50-53 and Burke, 1910, p. 137.
[152] Chateaubriand, 1849, p. 281. See also Compagnon, 2005, p. 81.

convolution (*Faltung*[153]) – i.e. an integral which "blends" two functions in order to express their dialectical relationship via a third function. It might be said that the antimoderns blend the function "past" with the function "present" to produce the function "antimodern". This dialectical balance echoes the thoughts of Walter Benjamin, whose project connected to the principles of montage and transformation, as described by Warburg in *Mnemosyne*. Benjamin pursued the avant-garde chasing 'the revolutionary energies that appear in the "outmoded" (*Veralteten*)'. He, moreover, expressed the ways these revolutionary energies survive conceptualising the notion of *dialectical image*.[154]

Dialectical images may be caused by transformations. They continuously encapsulate their own history – namely their births, rebirths and destructions, that is why the symbol of the *dialectical image* is an antique torso emerging from ruins according to Benjamin.[155] As such, the dialectical image does not merely interpret the past in the light of the present and vice versa:

> [...] rather, [it] is that wherein what has been comes together in a flash with the now to form a constellation. In other words, image is dialectics at a standstill. For while the relation of the *present* to the *past* is a purely temporal, continuous one, the relation of *what-has-been* to the *now* is dialectical: is not progression but image [...]. – Only dialectical images are genuine images (that is, not archaic).[156]

In the dialectical image, the *past* becomes *what-has-been*

---

[153] In German, *Faltung* also means *fold* in the geological sense of the word. A simplified mental representation of this phenomenon could be described as follows: a whole whose distinct parts move synchronically, mingle and become deformed because of the same external factor. This phenomenon could symbolise artistic creation. The artist, or the *creator* to speak like Nietzsche, might set the whole history of art in motion when painting, drawing, sculpting, writing or composing. In sum, a real and radical *displacement* occurs.
[154] See Rampley, 2000, pp. 33, 110 and Benjamin, 1977, p. 299.
[155] Didi-Huberman, 1992, pp. 129-130 and Benjamin, 2002, p. 340.
[156] Benjamin, 1999, p. 462.

while the *present* becomes the *now*. Benjamin thus acknowledged the dynamic nature of an artwork, which is torn between *what-has-been* and the *now*. *Some-thing-from-the-past* (or *the-present*) is not subordinated to the historical period in which it emerged but can be above it and permanently contemporary, or, out of time. Thus the modern artwork is neither absolutely new nor the repetition of the past, that is why the dialectical image is authentic, not archaic: it is not re(tro)gressive.[157]

Antimodern paintings are dialectical images like Ad Reinhardt's black paintings, which are 'imageless icons' embedded in negative theology.[158] It is because Twombly could solely paint Classical Antiquity in a new manner that Damisch described him as an archeologist, whose works are a cultural anamnesis.[159] Indeed, for the Christian Church, the anamnesis is not the commemoration but the endless revitalisation of the idea of Redemption, through an ever-renewed form.

Benjamin's dialectical image actually fed into his conception of historical time, which he developed from a reassessment of historical materialism underpinned by Jewish messianism. For Benjamin, historical time is 'saturated with moments of "now", whose intensity can, at any moment, interrupt the continuing temporality of historicity.'[160] He thus understood the artwork as an essentially ahistorical entity, which is not subordinated to the causality of a temporal process. His conception of the "present" consequently 'rescues the work of art from historical determinism and any kind of "people's history".'[161]

Benjamin's time, which seems to be antimodern, is nonetheless melancholic, despite its messianism.[162] But this melancholy is not Freudian and its definition is not given by, say, the *Oxford Dictionary*. The antimoderns' melancholy

---

[157] Didi-Huberman, 1992, pp. 138-139, 148.
[158] *Ibid.*, 1992, pp. 149-152.
[159] Damisch, 'Quant au titre. Cy Twombly' in Damisch, 2016, p. 57.
[160] Arasse, 2001, p. 216.
[161] *Ibid.*, pp. 218, 220.
[162] *Ibid.*, p. 216.

is the one of Renaissance humanism, epitomised by Dürer's *Melencolia I* in 1514 (Figure 23). Two of the characteristics defined by Panofsky resonate with antimodernity. The melancholics, like the antimoderns, 'think in terms of concrete mental images and not of abstract philosophical concepts': they are not theoreticians but artists.[163] They pursue what Dürer calls "consummate mastery" (*Gewalt*), that is to say, the perfect equivalence between practical skill (*Brauch*) and theoretical insight (*Kunst*).[164] This equivalence is indeed characteristic of antimodern painting, which conveys knowledge that relates to the painter's *métier* (as described by Lévi-Strauss), or, as Rilke would say, to what has been remoulded by age after age (*das von Geschlecht zu Geschlechtern gestaltet*) – think of Baselitz, Balthus, Twombly, Guston, or Bacon.[165] But one of the most eloquent elements in Dürer's *Melencolia I* might be Melancholia's wings. She is 'winged, yet cowering on the ground'[166] and echoes Baselitz's *Adler*: they both 'walk [....] way above the level of ordinary mortals'[167] and are yet condemned to live among them, like Baudelaire's albatross (*Exilé sur le sol au milieu des huées, / Ses ailes de géant l'empêchent de marcher*).[168]

The antimoderns of the 1970s painted the melancholic fusion of *what-has-been* and the *now*, raising themselves above historical continuity. Their works are traditional with hints of modernity or modern with hints of tradition. In this light, maybe shall we reconsider Warhol's portraits to see them as a series of homages in the manner of Botticelli? Think

[163] Panofsky, 1945, p. 168.
[164] *Ibid.*, p. 164.
[165] See Lévi-Strauss, 1981 and Rilke, 1942, pp. 86-87. On the difficulty to translate 'Geschlecht' in an accurate and proper manner, see Derrida, 2008, p. 51: 'I am not sure that one can speak of *Geschlecht* beyond the word "Geschlecht" – which is then necessarily cited, between quotation marks, mentioned rather than used. And I leave the word in German. As I have already said, no word, no word for word will suffice to translate this word that gathers, in its idiomatic meaning, stock, race, family, species, genus, generation, sex.' See also Krell quoted in Derrida, 2008, pp. 59-60.
[166] Panofsky, 1945, p. 168.
[167] *Ibid.*, p. 165.
[168] Baudelaire, 1954, p. 86.

of Warhol's *Ileana Sonnabend*[169] (Figure 24) and Botticelli's *Giuliano de Medici* (Figure 25). Either way, the antimoderns looked both backward and forward, or, as Barthes once said: '[their] own historical position was to be at the rear-guard of the avant-garde: to be avant-garde one must know what is dead; to be rear-guard, one must still love it...'[170] We should now remember that modernity was born against the modern world: its very essence is embedded in traditions and classicism, oriented towards an innovative creative process, *contra* any form of academicism. The antimoderns, for their part, are what the French call *passeurs*: they remember things past.

I placed this essay under the sign of André Malraux... and it seems that the antimoderns are the Malrucian elephants: newborns in a fresh world, neither young nor old, they ruminate their past lives.

---

[169] This portrait was hung in one of the galleries surrounding the main gallery, which included Balthus's, Baselitz's and de Kooning's works.
[170] Barthes, 2002, p. 1038 (my trans.)

ATLAS

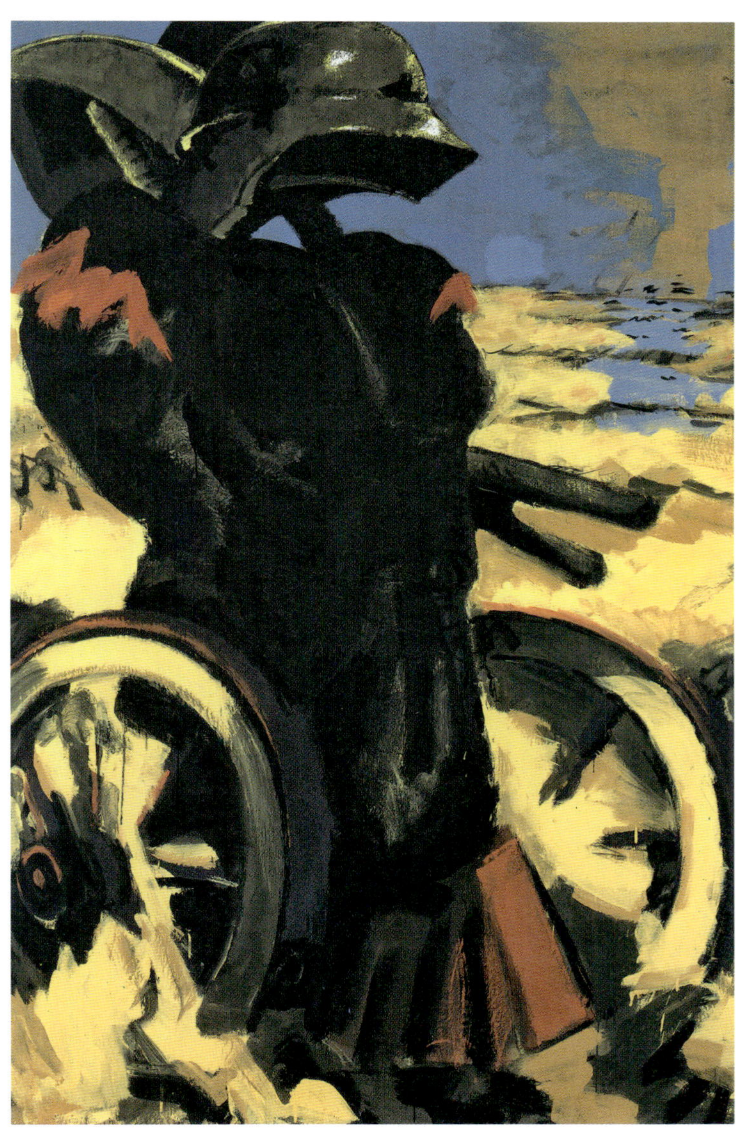

1 Markus Lüpertz, *Schwarz-Rot-Gold dithyrambisch I*, 1974

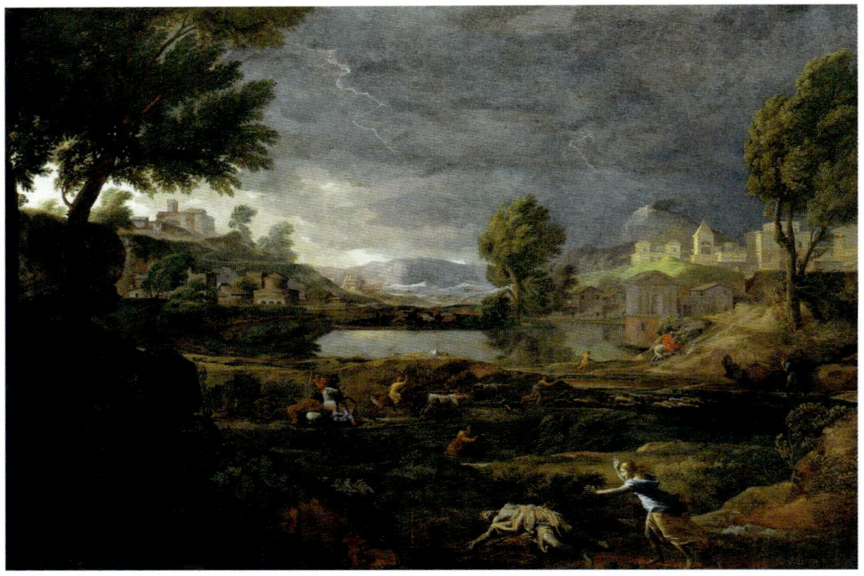

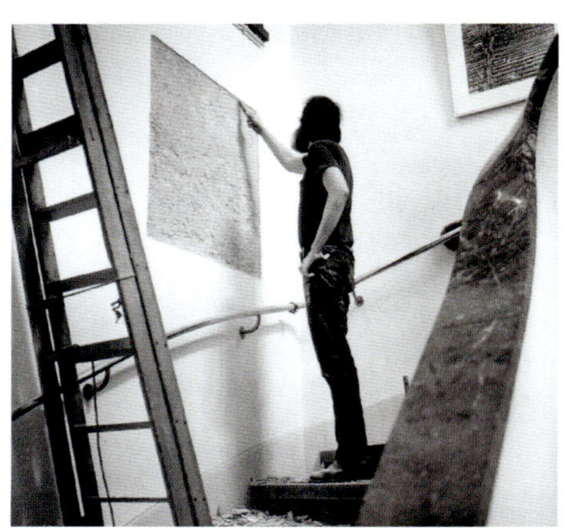

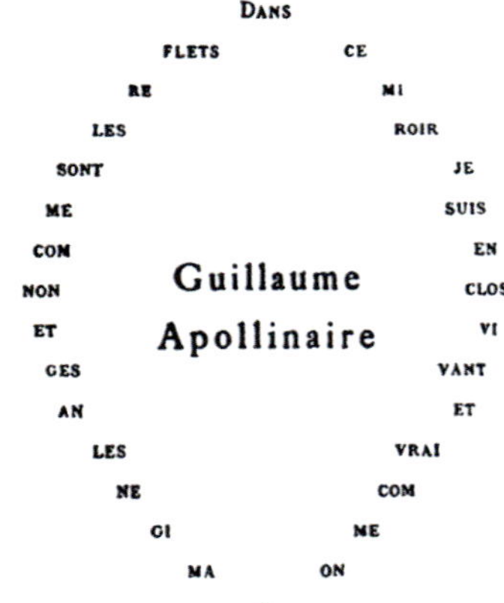

2 Guillaume Apollinaire, 'Cœur, Couronne et Miroir' in *Calligrammes*, 1918

3 Nicolas Poussin, *Paysage de tempête avec Pyrame et Thisbé*, 1641

4 Lawrence Weiner constructing *36" X 36" Removal to the Lathing or Support Wall of Plaster or Wallboard from a Wall* for 'When Attitudes Become Form', Kunsthalle Bern, 1969

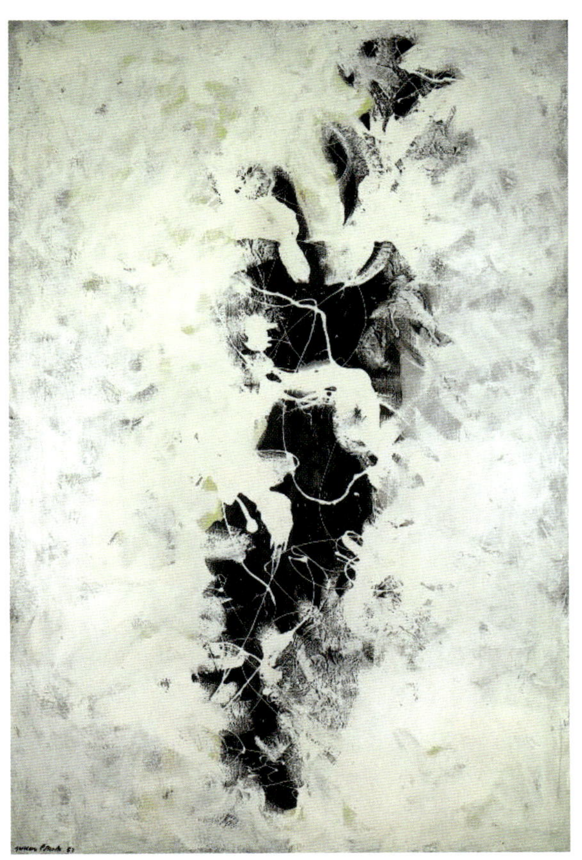

5 Jackson Pollock, *The Deep*, 1953

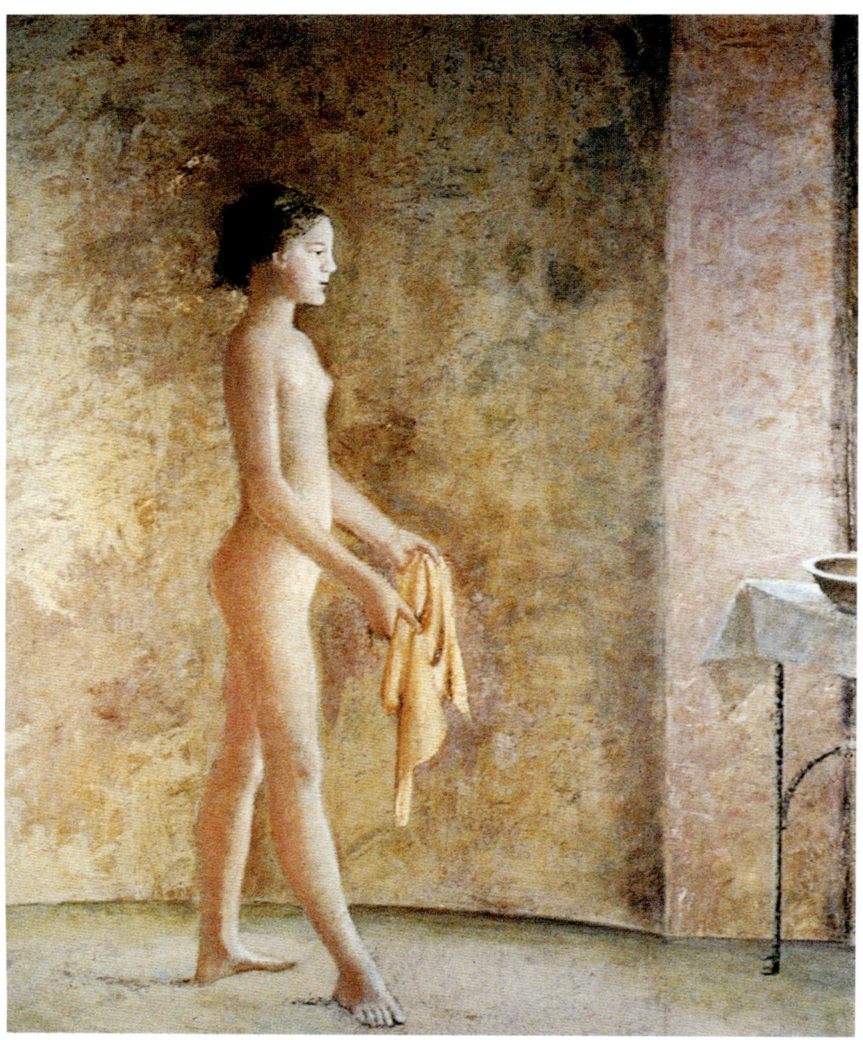

6 Balthus, *Nu de profil*, 1973-1977

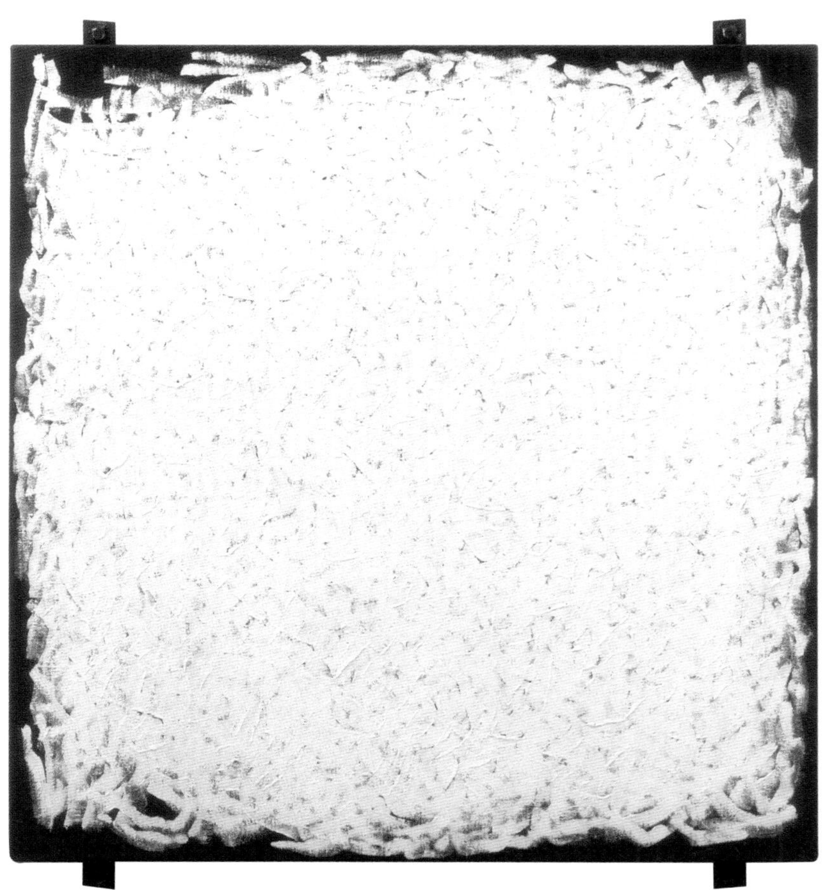

(7) Robert Ryman, *Unit*, 1980

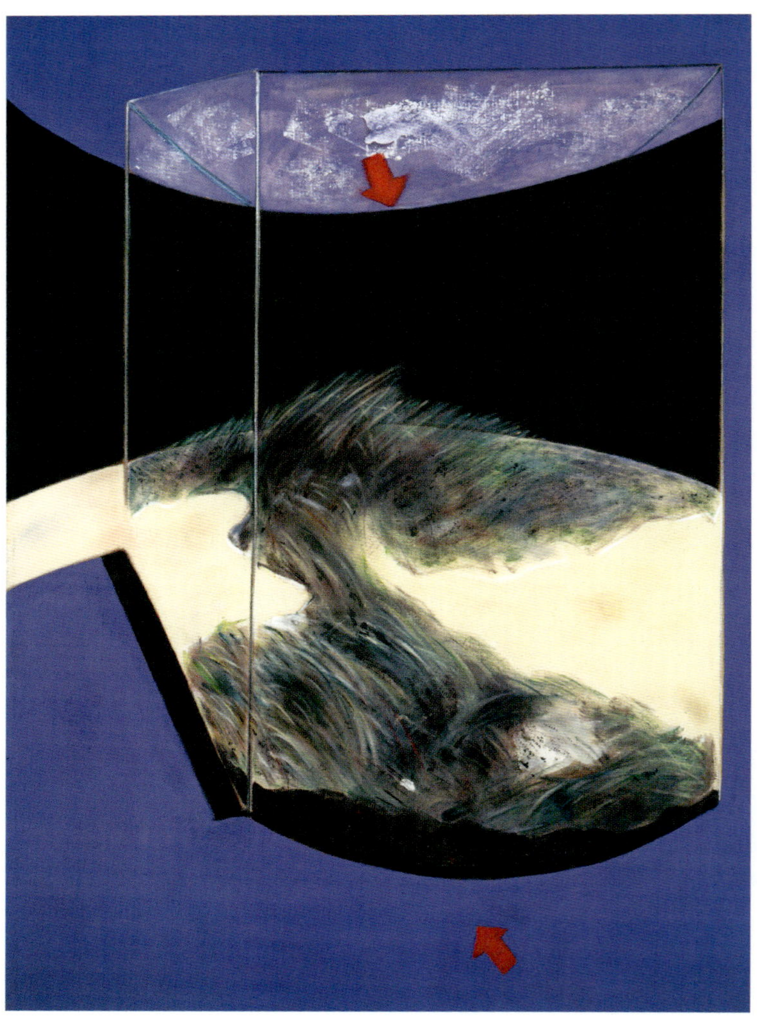

(8) Francis Bacon, *Landscape*, 1978

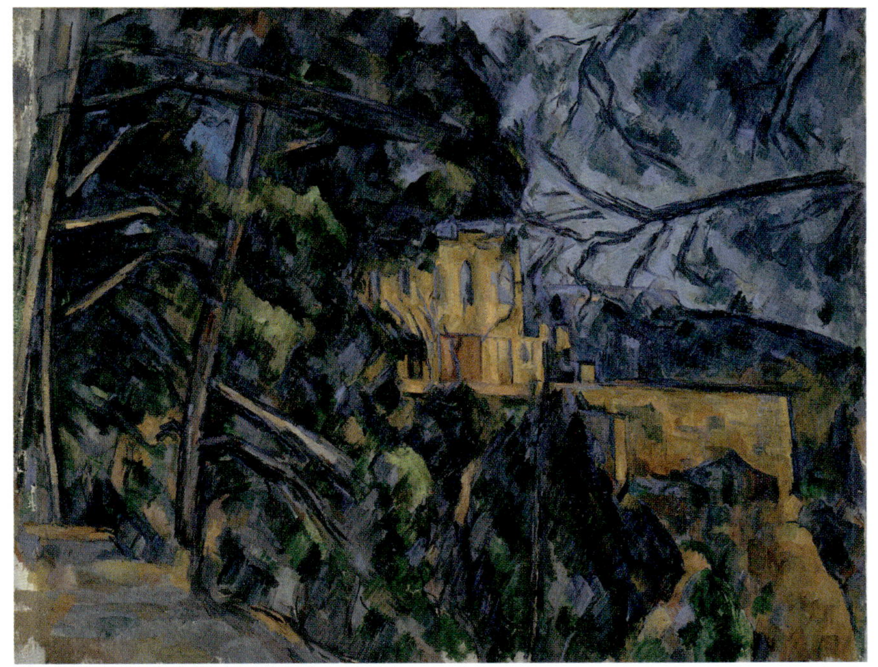

9 Paul Cézanne, *Château noir*, 1900-1904

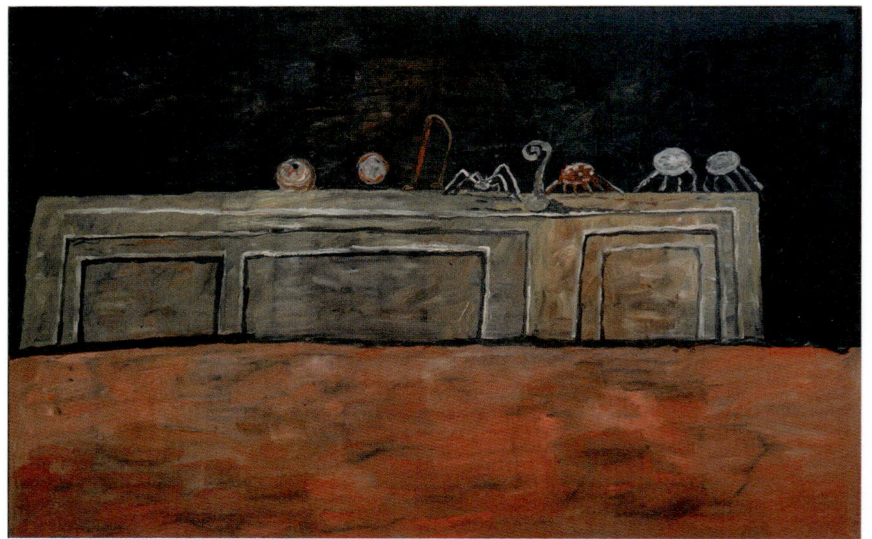

(10) Philip Guston, *Door*, 1978

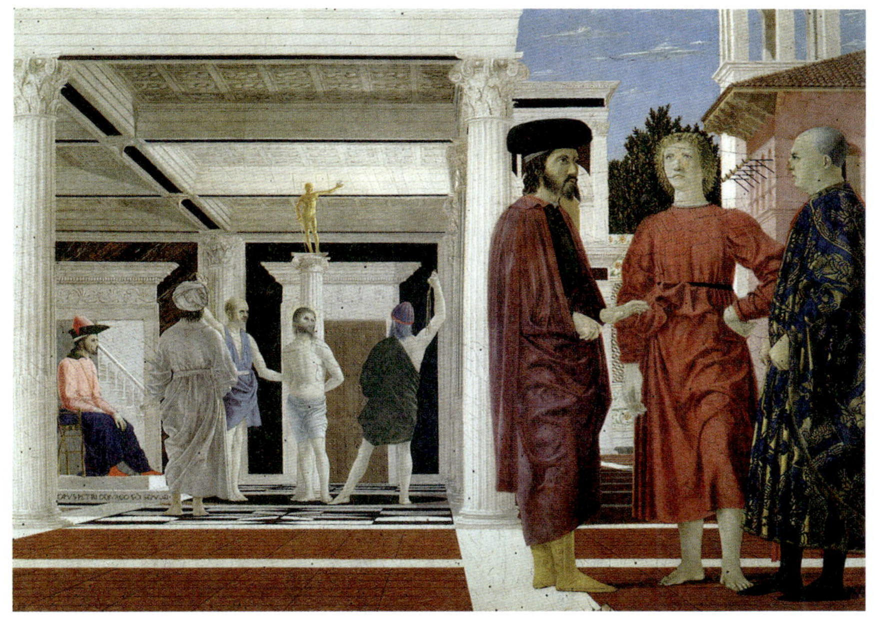

11 Piero della Francesca, *Flagellazione*, 1459-1460

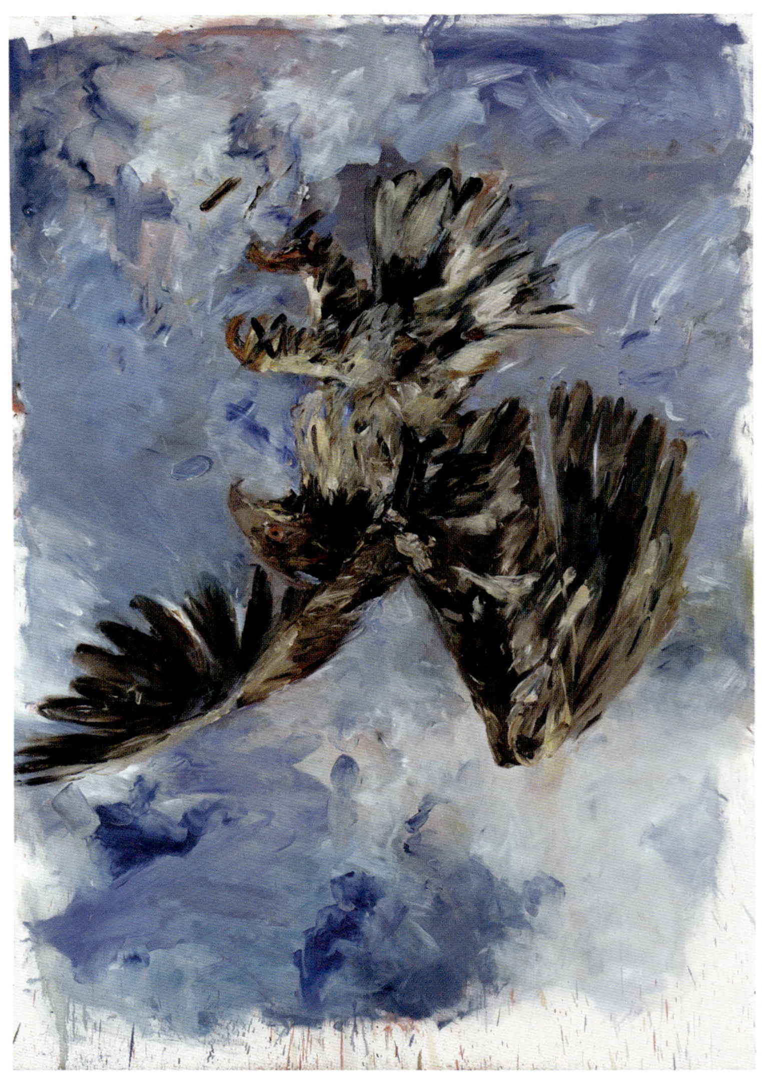

(12) Georg Baselitz, *Fingermalerei-Adler*, 1972

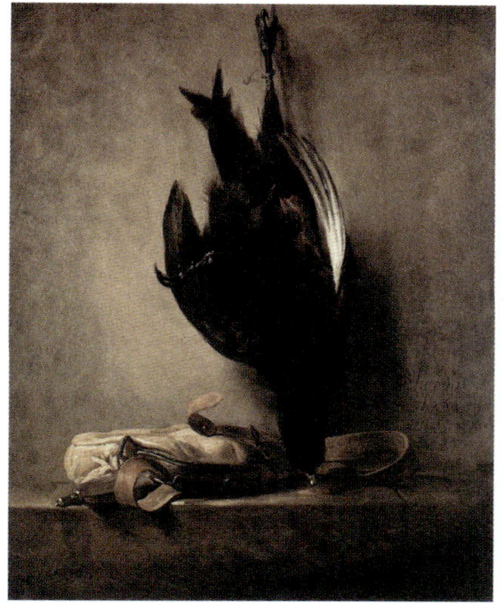

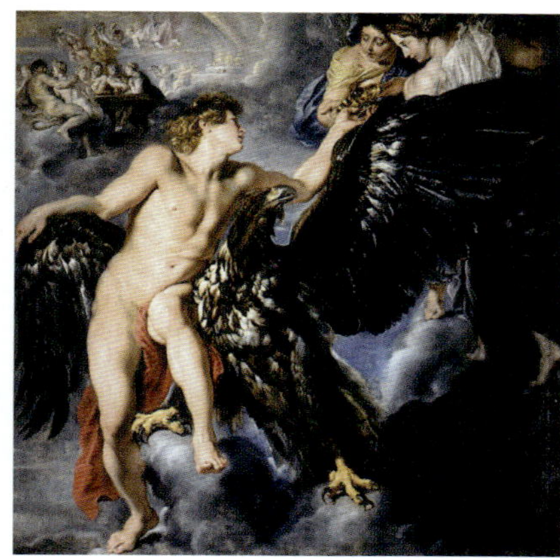

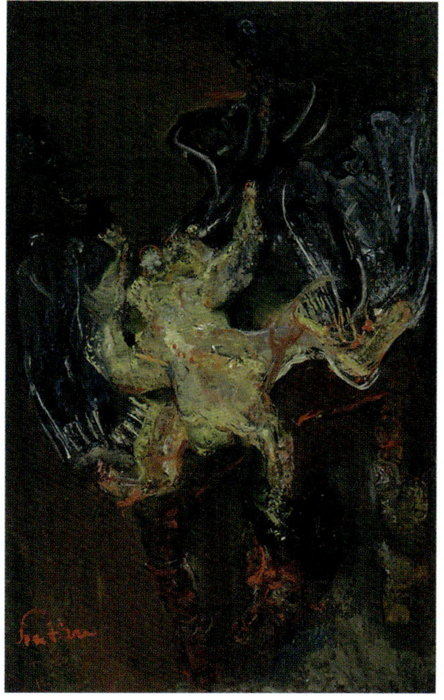

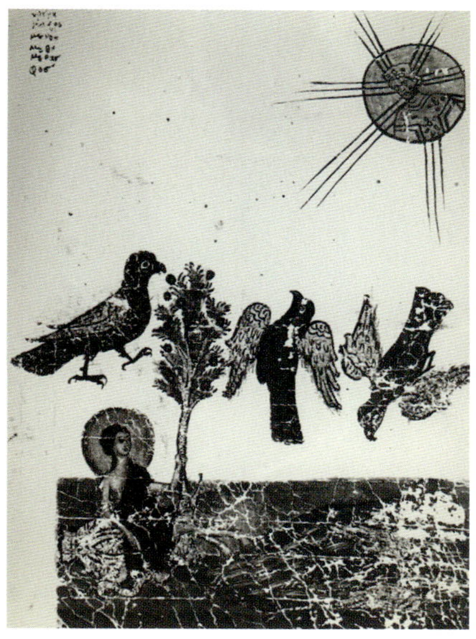

13 Jean Siméon Chardin, *Nature morte au faisan et gibecière*, 1760
14 Chaïm Soutine, *Dead Fowl*, 1926
15 Peter Paul Rubens, *The Abduction of Ganymede*, 1611-1612
16 *Smyrna Physiologus*, Twelfth Century AD

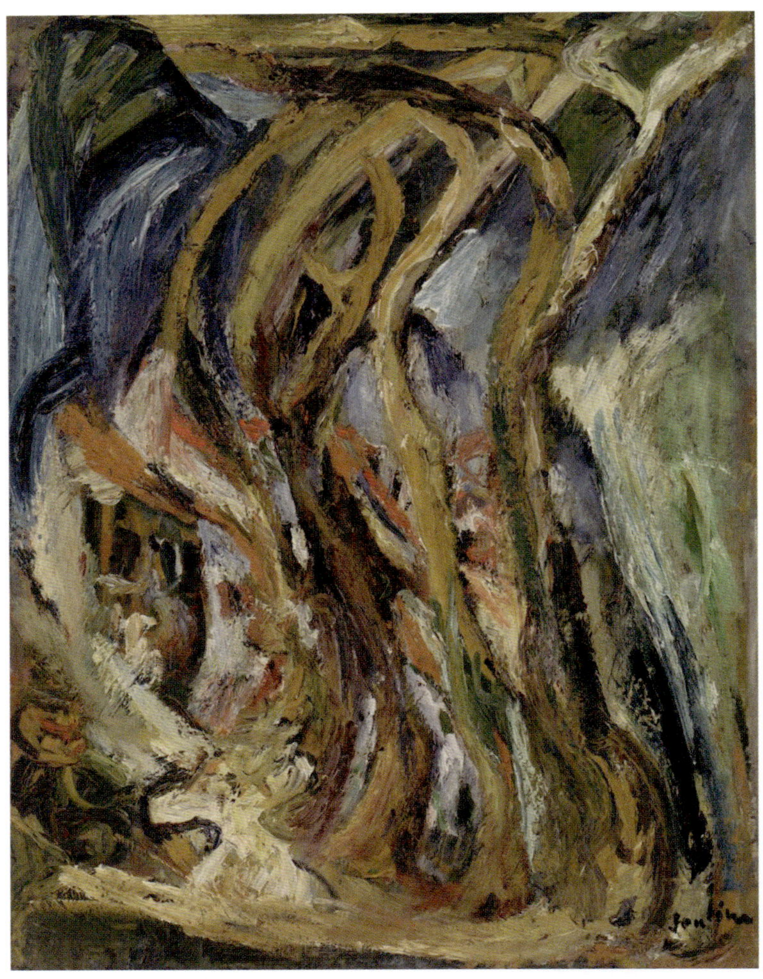

17 Chaïm Soutine, *Groupe d'arbres*, 1922

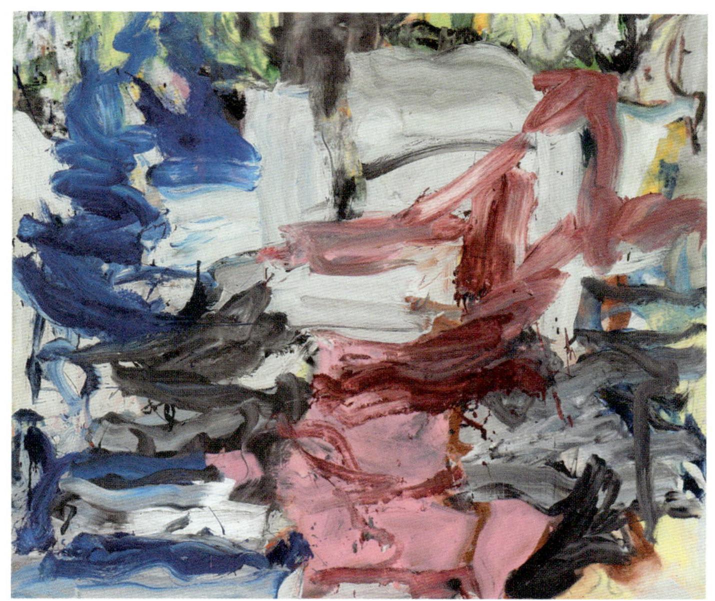

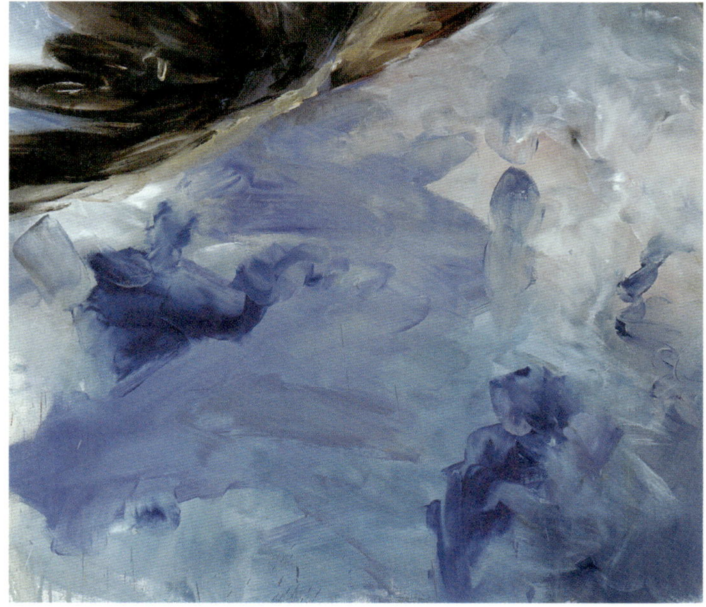

(18) Willem de Kooning, *Untitled II*, 1977
(19) Georg Baselitz, *Fingermalerei-Adler* (detail), 1972

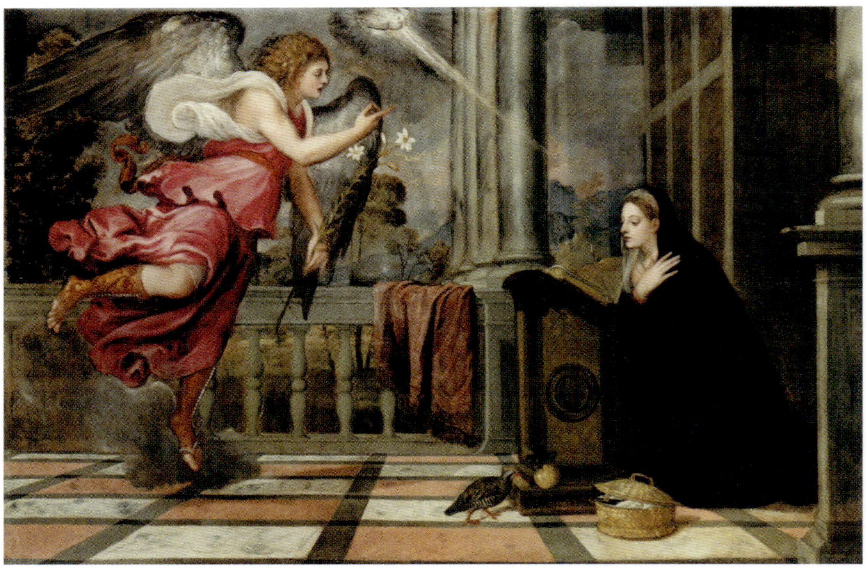

(20) Gerhard Richter, *Verkündigung nach Tizian* (344-3), 1973
21 Tiziano, *Annunciazione*, 1535

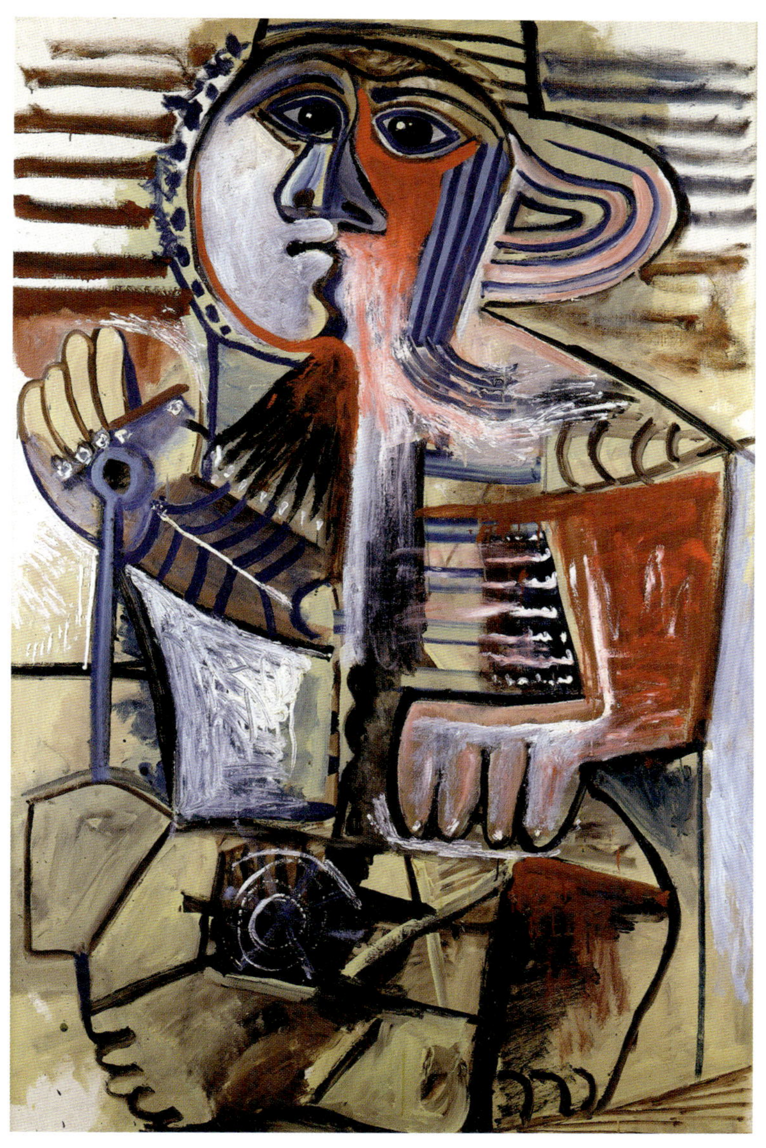

(22) Pablo Picasso, *Child with a Spade*, 1971

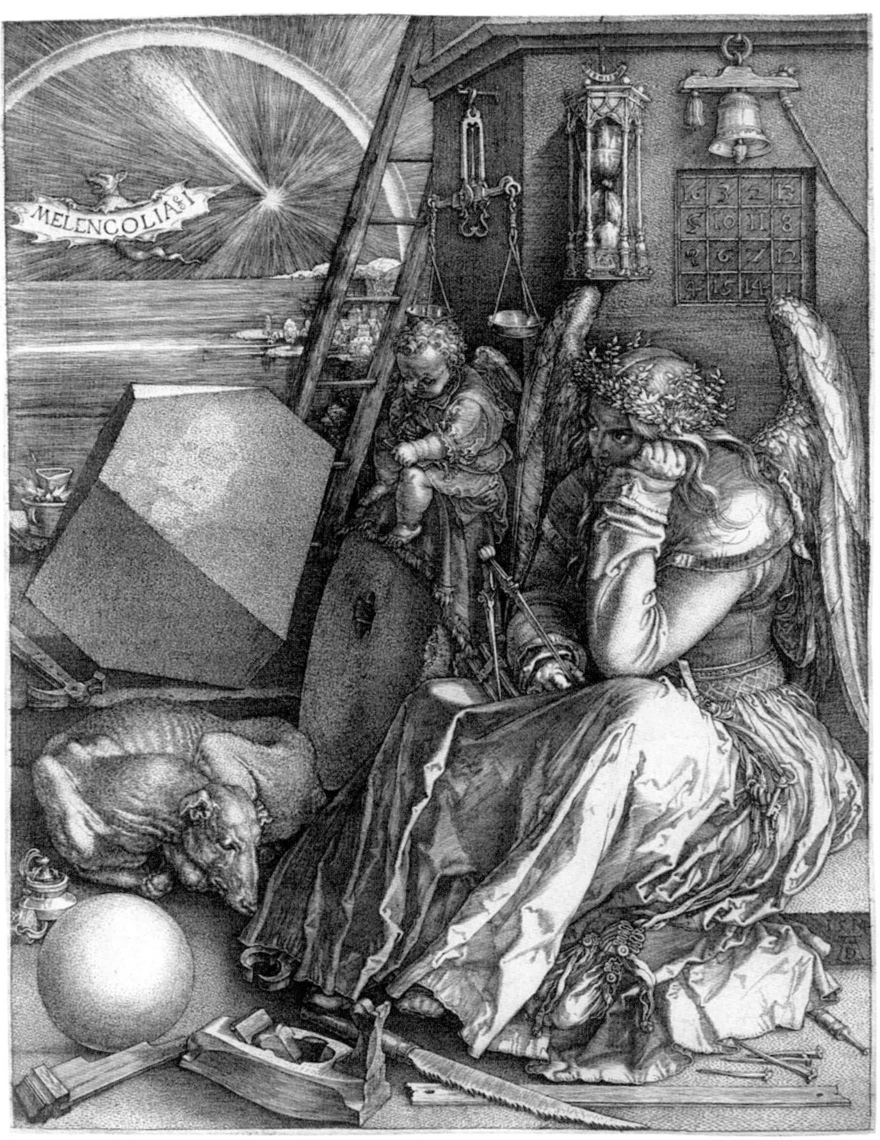

23 Albrecht Dürer, *Melencolia I*, 1514

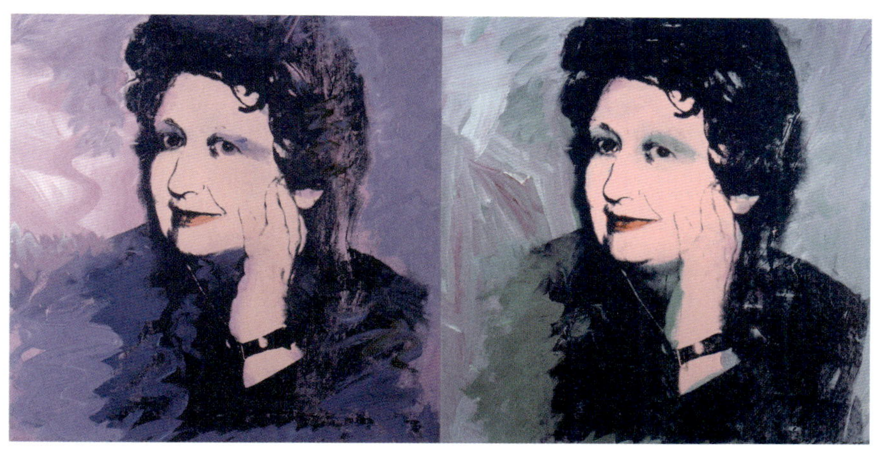

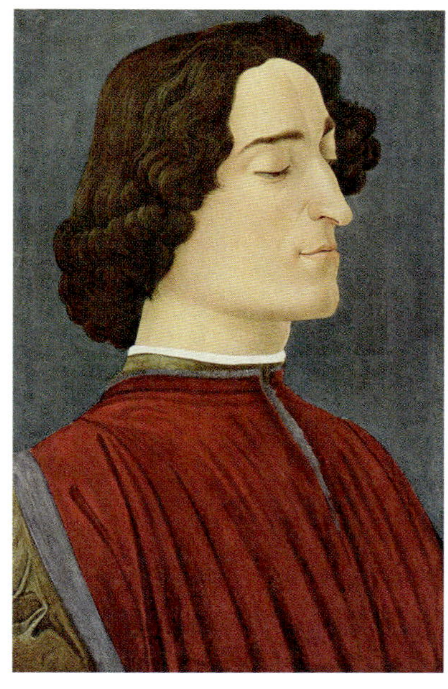

(24) Andy Warhol, *Ileana Sonnabend*, 1973
25 Sandro Botticelli, *Giuliano de' Medici*, 1478

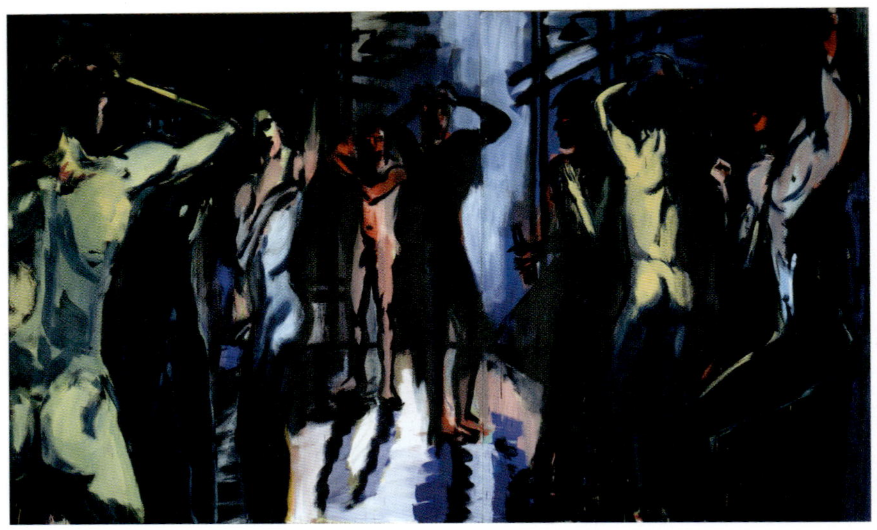

26 Rainer Fetting, *Große Dusche (Panorama)*, 1981

INTERVIEWS

THÉO DE LUCA
IN CONVERSATION WITH:

Norman Rosenthal
in conversation with Théo de Luca
Soho, London, United Kingdom

16 October 2017
11 December 2017
7 January 2019

Théo de Luca *I see 'A New Spirit in Painting' as a constellation or a cosmology. Different groups of painters can actually be identified in it. The German painters, the Italian painters, what I call the American-European painters, the "Old Masters" and so on. What was your role in bringing this constellation together? How did this constellation come together?*

Norman Rosenthal In 1974, I did what seemed to me at the time a big show at the ICA. So I had these two options: to do an exhibition about Beuys and his world, or an exhibition about Baselitz and his world. The ICA was too small to do both. So I chose to do Beuys and his world. I would have loved to do Baselitz and his world but I had to make a choice. So when I had this idea to do the show at the Royal Academy, the idea was to do an exhibition that would place Baselitz in a big international context. It was the *nouveauté* because everybody knew Balthus, everybody knew de Kooning... In the Royal Academy's main gallery, there was Baselitz, Balthus – aspiring as he was to be the Piero della Francesca of our time, and de Kooning – like the maximum of American painterly Abstract Expressionism. I could have put Guston in this room but de Kooning was more relevant to Baselitz. It's kind of interesting that later on Baselitz was to do a lot of paintings in homage to de Kooning. This was the centre piece of the exhibition and everything was around it. There were further important things. One was the constellation of Francis Bacon and Philip Guston. The other incredibly important thing was the rediscovery of the late Picasso in that exhibition. Those were the most important things.

TdL *It seems that much paintings from the show were out of time, and somehow acting counter to our time, for the benefit of a time to come.*

NR All those painters were not in the norm of that moment. Picasso was not in the norm of that moment. Bacon was not in the norm of that moment. Philip Guston was not in the norm of that moment. Schnabel was not in the norm of that moment. Even Stella was not in the norm of that moment because if you thought of Stella and closed your eyes, what you thought of was these big black abstract paintings of the 1960s.

TdL *It looks like the exhibition staged a certain society and thus conveyed a certain idea of what painting should be. For example, Warhol's paintings portrayed people connected to 'A New Spirit in Painting': Ileana Sonnabend, Hélène Rochas...*

NR Of course, Hélène Rochas was the lender of some of the paintings by Balthus. Ileana because she was Ileana, the great dealer of that time. David Hockney because he was David Hockney and so it goes on.

TdL *Looking back, a genealogy can be unfolded. Decisive exhibitions took place before 'A New Spirit in Painting'. One could think of the exhibitions organised at the Kunstmuseum Basel or the Whitechapel. The 1980 Venice Biennale was crucial as well...*

NR Of course! A lot of information came by the Venice Biennale. We all went there. You know it was in the air. Julian Schnabel was the mediator to America of people like Polke, Richter and Baselitz. Julian was the man who brought the news of European painting to America. It was we who tried to bring the news in a much bigger way to an international platform, and maybe we succeeded.

TdL *Did you endeavour to outstrip the New York art world?*

NR Yes! We wanted to break out of the New York hegemony. And I suppose it's the beginning of what you might call a new 'World Art' – that's why it was a revolution! It led to a huge expansion in the people's perception of the legitimacy of art being not just in New York – and maybe in London, from an Anglo-Saxon perspective. I remember the rest of the world didn't exist. There was no Africa, there was no South

America, there was no Australia, there was no South East Asia, there was no Middle East. That didn't come in. That was yet to come!

TdL *Conceptually, how close were 'A New Spirit in Painting' and your project on the masterpieces from the Gemäldegalerie Alte Meister Kassel? To what extent are they related?*

NR They are only related by accident. You know everything happens by chance. The Kassel project was intended for the Royal Academy. At that point, I wasn't thinking about some groundbreaking exhibition, what I call culturally groundbreaking exhibition of contemporary art. The other thing is: it's much quicker of course to do a contemporary art exhibition, through not easier. What I discovered there quickly is that to do what I call historical exhibitions takes several years but to do a contemporary art exhibition, it's much better to be quick. If you spend too much time thinking about it, then the time is gone and you are already kind of *passé*. In order to be not *passé*, but *au courant*, you have to be quick. What I call the art world of today is not going to be the same in a year's time, whereas Rembrandt is going to be basically the same next year.

I had eleven months to do it so I had to move very quickly. The ruling elite of the Royal Academy was, at that time, connected to the Royal College of Art. They were teachers there and also connected with a kind of establishment. The President of the Royal Academy, Sir Hugh Casson, was also one the main instigators of something called the Festival of Britain in 1951 – all the South Bank was invented at that time. He wasn't very *au courant* with contemporary art. There was also a number of teachers who were on the Royal Academy committee, like Roger de Grey or Carel Weight, many of whom appear in a famous painting by Rodrigo Moynihan, who really wanted to be in 'A New Spirit in Painting'. Rodrigo Moynihan was a contemporary of Francis Bacon in the 1930s and later became quite a conservative painter.

The other person who was desperate to be in 'A New Spirit in Painting' was Lawrence Gowing, who painted very much in the manner of Roger Fry – who invented Post-Impressionism, before the First World War, and was very connected with Bloomsbury. I went off to Gowing's studio. He was at the time the head of the Slade School of Art. He got all these naked ladies to lie on canvases, like Yves Klein. He thought that he was doing something *nouveau*. So I had to tell him that what I call his Yves Klein-like paintings were not exactly what I wanted to show.

Also, a very famous art dealer in London at that time, Robert Fraser, and a friend of his, Brian Clarke – who looks after the estate of Francis Bacon today, took me to see some new painters. I saw these less than original abstract geometrical paintings. They thought they could persuade me to include these artists in the show. I had to resist quite hard because, at that time, I was the new boy. I had to find strategies to resist them.

So I've suddenly found myself in this rather old fashioned kind of world, that has rather connections with a kind of modernism before the First World War, that's the world they lived in. The Academicians Hugh Casson, Roger de Grey, and Frederick Gore – who was a painter taught at Saint Martins and the son of an English early modernist painter, Spencer Gore – told me: 'Go to New York, go and see Ileana Sonnabend and Leo Castelli, bring *l'art américain* to London in a big exhibition.' But I wanted to do something different, that's why I did the show with some German artists, but also some Italian artists – Palladino and the world of what they called the three C's (Cucchi, Clemente and Sandro Chia), or Jannis Kounellis who was a friend of Christos. Jannis Kounellis especially painted pictures for us. They were very good and strong. He's a great artist and, of course, again, then almost unknown.

TdL *Can you say more about the year before 'A New Spirit in Painting'?*

NR Yes! The year before 'A New Spirit in Painting', I had helped organise the most successful exhibition ever of the Royal Academy: 'Post-Impressionism'. We made a model for the reinterpretation of late nineteenth-century French art. I remember Michel Laclotte and the young curator Henri Loyrette, who later became Director of the Louvre, coming to London and discussing with us our theories about French art. My colleagues on this project wanted to concentrate on artists like Henri Martin and all these sorts of symbolist people. But I also included amazing pictures by the great artists, which they rather resented. Gauguin, van Gogh, late Monet and so on. So the art historians were not that interested in those painters. That was a big success and that gave me my initial strength. They began to trust me.

TdL *But several Royal Academicians, for example, Eduardo Paolozzi, were against 'A New Spirit in Painting'.*

NR What I call the modern artists of the Academy, like John Hoyland and Eduardo Paolozzi, were very much connected to certain galleries in London: Waddington but also the Marlborough Gallery. There was a connection between the dealers and certain artists. The chief artists who were against me were John Hoyland, Peter Blake and Eduardo Paolozzi. But also certain artists who were even included in the exhibition, like David Hockney, Ron Kitaj and Howard Hodgkin, who felt that their position in the art world was threatened by those new names.

TdL *Who were the new names?*

NR Baselitz, Kiefer, Richter… all these people!

TdL *What did you think of painters like Peter Halley, who said one can no longer spend one hour looking at a painting by Cézanne?*

NR Peter Halley was later. He is the epoch of Jeff Koons, like five years later. In America, we are talking about the epoch of people like the Pictures generation and their contemporary painters like David Salle and Julian Schnabel, who was the big star in New York at that time.
But this "new painting" thing did not last very long. The big

star of 'A New Spirit in Painting', even more than Baselitz, was Rainer Fetting. In 1981, Anthony d'Offay was much more keen on Rainer Fetting. He deserves a real revival, I think.

TdL *Was the idea of focusing on painting related to the fact that Royal Academicians are elected for their preeminence in one of the four categories – painting, sculpture, printmaking, architecture?*

NR Yes it was. The interesting thing is that the exhibition nearly did not take place. Two nights before the opening, I was with Christos Joachimides and Nicholas Serota in the galleries. It was almost midnight and we were still hanging the exhibition. We were behind the doors and suddenly there was a big knocking... I was in there with David Sylvester, because he wasn't going to press viewings and he wanted to see the exhibition ahead of time. He was a friend of Nicholas Serota, Christos Joachimides and me. Ron Kitaj, David Hockney, Vera Russell – who was a grand dame of the English art world, with whom I worked as a young man and who thought I was betraying British Art as did Bryan Robertson – and, I think, Howard Hodgkin came to take their paintings down, which of course would have been a big scandal. It was only David Sylvester who prevented this to happen. He sort of said: 'this is a very important exhibition, you must not do this.'

There was also this big thing with Peter Blake and John Hoyland who tried to get the exhibition not to open. They accused me, with Leslie Waddington in the background, of being in the pay of Michael Werner, to the extent that they called a meeting with all the members of the Royal Academy, within twenty-four hours, and they voted whether the exhibition should be allowed to open. All the conservative members of the Royal Academy approved the exhibition, and all the so-called progressive ones, like Paolozzi, Peter Blake, the, at that time, sort of avant-garde artists, were against it because they felt threatened. In the end, they were right to feel threatened because it undermined their Anglo-American position.

At that time, I was not Sir Norman, I was little Norman, the young new curator. I had huge success the year before with

the 'Post-Impressionism' exhibition. But with 'A New Spirit in Painting', I could have lost my job, that's why I asked Nicholas Serota to be part of the team. He had a kind of gravitas that I did not have. It is not about who we were but how we were perceived. People regarded Nicholas Serota as a kind of serious person destined to be the director of the Tate.
It's still the most important exhibition I have ever done. If you look at Roger Fry's 'Manet and the Post-Impressionists' show in 1910, if you look at what was in it, there are some stupid things too. But it still doesn't take away from the fundamental push. History is a very cool judge.

TdL *How was your relationship with Christos Joachimides?*

NR Christos was the person who introduced me to the art of Europe. He studied with Heidegger and had lived in Rome and Paris. He knew all kind of people around there: Jannis Kounellis, the Arte povera people, the young and the old German artists... I was able to enter Germany and what I call the axis Rome-Paris because of him. At the time, I was thirty-three and he was forty-five. That's a big difference! He had an experience which I couldn't have had. He knew Balthus when he was at the Villa Medici and introduced me to him. To do exhibitions you have to have access to artists. But the big stars of that time in Europe were Rudi Fuchs and Harry Szeemann. Christos was thought to be a slightly marginal figure. In a way, he was a sort of a marginal figure and even acted as a marginal figure. It was more a question of character and a question of knowing how to play the art world. You have to know how to play the art world, which I did but he didn't.

TdL *Can you say more about 'Zeitgeist'?*

NR 'Zeitgeist' is the baroque version of 'A New Spirit in Painting'. Neither of the shows were perfect but they did demonstrate a kind of change in the art world. Also, they brought a big change in the whole business of collecting. If I hadn't done it, somebody else would have done it. The fact was that the Royal Academy was a very unexpected venue and so was the venue of Berlin as well. Until then, Berlin was rather marginal to the art world compared to Düsseldorf and Cologne. Suddenly, Berlin became a capital for the first time. The Royal Academy was the least likely place on the entire planet for this exhibition to take place. It had prestige. If the exhibition had been at the Tate Gallery, it wouldn't have had the same impact.

TdL *There were no women artists in the show. Why not include women artists who painted in the same vein at that time?*

NR I'm doing an exhibition about 'A New Spirit in Painting' in New York with Almine Rech, but I can't do without women artists. In 'Zeitgeist', we had Susan Rothenberg. But the artist I most regret not including is Maria Lassnig. I knew her work, kind of regret now not including her.

Also, I didn't include Basquiat. I could have included Basquiat. Maybe now, in retrospective, it was a mistake not to include him. He's an unbelievably talented artist but somehow, when I met him in New York, all I could see was this image of this boy being fed with drugs, like a caged animal. I met him in his studio in Soho. At that time Chelsea didn't exist. The center of the art world was West Broadway and the streets of West Broadway, both in terms of galleries and studios. Also, the art criticism world as led by the magazine *October* and the person of Rosalind Krauss, for whom art was just a long journey towards immateriality. 'A New Spirit in Painting' was obviously a challenge which she would never accept. But to return to Basquiat, I remember going to this basement, I think in Prince Street, where he seemed to me like an animal in a cage. I was alas not radical enough to understand the significance anyway of people from what I call the graffiti world like Keith Harring. Now and looking back, the Basquiat had incredible talent. Actually, he now can be seen as a great post-Twombly artist. I can only see that now. But you can't see everything. I had my vision and my matrix was Baselitz. He was the matrix that I was trying to mediate at that time. And funnily enough, I would say still, forty years later, he has still not quite achieved the acceptance of many of the artists in that show. He has not achieved the acceptance of Basquiat. He has not achieved the acceptance of Anselm Kiefer. He has not received quite the acceptance of Richter and Polke

TdL *How would you explain that Baselitz has not achieved the acceptance of the other German artists (Kiefer, Richter, Polke...)?*

NR You know it has to do with the American taste. Of course, he has fame. Of course, he sells pictures. Of course, people like him. But especially in America, the museum culture has not bought into him in the way they have bought into the other German artists. In the end, the Museum of Modern Art has not really bought into him because the Museum of Modern Art is still a kind of a temple. If you have a show at the Museum of Modern Art, you've arrived. It's one of the destinations, even today. Some things take time, some things happen later. It's the way of the world. I have my subjective taste too, so maybe I'm wrong but I don't think I am.

TdL *What's your subjective taste?*

NR I've just been to see the Jasper Johns exhibition and of course Johns is a fantastic painter. Baselitz is someone that I would put next to someone like Jasper Johns. For me, one of the most cultivated and interesting painters of the second half of the twentieth century is definitely Baselitz – for me the Picasso of his generation – a pure painter when others are "artists". He survives the taste of time. But that's my opinion, it's still quite difficult.

TdL *Why was Jasper Johns not included in the show? What if you had the possibility to make a second version of the show?*

NR Time. Time changes things. It was the time when Jasper Johns did these crosshatching paintings. At that time, I thought they were completely superficial and stupid. Now, I think they're absolutely wonderful. But then, I was so into Baselitz that I could not see the quality of those paintings. On the contrary, I thought he was an artist who lost the plot.

In fact, he hasn't lost the plot at all. He's one of the greatest artists of all time. He's like Cézanne, the level of Cézanne. I only realise that now.

In every exhibition there are mistakes. If I was to do it again, there are three or four things I would drop and three or four things I would include. That is to every group exhibition. If you can find any group exhibition after thirty years, you would do it a bit different because time is always changing things.

Thaddaeus Ropac in conversation with Théo de Luca Galerie Thaddaeus Ropac - Ely House Mayfair, London, United Kingdom

1 November 2017

Théo de Luca *What are your memories of 'A New Spirit in Painting' and 'Zeitgeist'? It seems that your gallery's programme has partly stemmed from these two exhibitions.*

Thaddaeus Ropac Going to London to see 'A New Spirit in Painting' was crucial. It was amazing! I was also an intern during 'Zeitgeist'. It was my beginning. It was and still is the most important show to me because I took part in it and I had not started my gallery at the time.

When were the shows? Which time of the year?

TdL *'A New Spirit in Painting' took place in 1981, from January to March. 'Zeitgeist' took place from October 1982 to January 1983.*

TR In 1981, I traveled to London to see 'A New Spirit in Painting' because I had heard about it. I'm sure it was the first time I saw works by Baselitz and Kiefer, which deeply impressed me. In 1982, I went to Düsseldorf to meet Beuys. I had the chance to go to Berlin with him, where I was an intern during the installation of 'Zeitgeist'. In 1983, I decided to open my gallery in Salzburg. Then, I started to work with many of the artists included in both shows. For example, I worked with Sandro Chia in the 1980s; he was important for me in the beginning. I had my first exhibitions with Penck and Baselitz right away. In 1982, I saw Warhol visiting 'Zeitgeist', in which he was included. I met with him a year later in New York and had a first small exhibition in 1984. I did shows with Lüpertz in 1983 and 1986. I asked Rainer Fetting to be part of an exhibition focused on Mozart as a metaphor for the arts, which I presented in Salzburg in 1985. I also got very close to Kirkeby since I got him a studio in Salzburg in the summer of 1985. Interestingly enough, a few artists participating in these two shows did not make a big career. You could not show the same artists together in a relevant way today. However, these exhibitions are of major importance for me. It was the beginning of a certain modernity, of a new era.

TdL *When did you first meet with Norman? How did you meet and eventually collaborate with the artists you have mentioned?*

TR I first met with Norman during 'Zeitgeist' in 1982. There, I was part of the installation team. It was great: Beuys invited me to Berlin, I was very young and I wanted to work, to look, to learn. I was first in Düsseldorf and then traveled to documenta and Berlin. I was very much part of this world in a way. When I later opened my gallery in 1983, I wrote to the artists whom I met during 'Zeitgeist' and people took me seriously. I wrote to Baselitz, to Kiefer, to Kirkeby, to many of them. I was able to use the connections I had through the show to contact the artists again and, somehow, Salzburg was an exotic place then. It helped in a way.

TdL *How did you manage to work with these artists? Baselitz, Kirkeby, Lüpertz and Penck were represented by Michael Werner in the 1980s.*

TR When I wrote to Baselitz, Kirkeby, Lüpertz and Penck, they replied that they would like to be part of my project but asked me to speak to Michael Werner first. So I worked with them through Michael Werner, he gave me access to them. The first steps had to be formal but it went into personal relationships afterwards. For example, as I have mentioned, I invited Kirkeby to spend the summer of 1985 in Salzburg where I got him a studio, then we showed in 1986 the paintings he had created there. I had the chance to meet great artists during these three weeks in Berlin. It led to many years of successful collaborations.

TdL *Regarding the eighties' art scene in Cologne, I was wondering whether you collaborated with Rudolf Zwirner.*

TR No, not really since Zwirner was more an art dealer, he was not so much a gallerist who represented artists. He did amazing exhibitions, which I visited and learned a lot from. I was more interested in a direct contact with artists. I wanted access to them.

TdL *Did Anthony d'Offay give you access to any of the artists you worked with?*

TR I met with him early because he was part of 'Zeitgeist' and represented many of these artists, including Anselm Kiefer. Through d'Offay, I was able to get works for my gallery to exhibit. Only much later I was able to meet Kiefer in his studio and to start a relationship which led to many successful exhibitions.

TdL *You organised the exhibition 'German Art: Aspekte deutscher Kunst 1964–1994' in 1994. It included many of the artists from 'A New Spirit in Painting' – Baselitz, Kiefer, Penck, Polke or Richter, but also artists such as Beuys or Knoebel. It was organised five years after the Guggenheim's exhibition on German art: 'Refigured Painting: The German Image 1960-88'. What about the message behind your exhibition did you want to convey?*

TR Wieland Schmied helped me curate the show. We tried to show aspects of German art from the mid-1960s to the mid-1990s. Of course, in each of these decades, Beuys's persona was one the central figures in Germany and beyond. In 1994, Beuys had to be the center of the exhibition. The way America looked at German art was actually driven by the experience of Beuys and the Beuys exhibition which took place at the Guggenheim in 1979.

Tim Marlow
in conversation with Théo de Luca
The Academicians' Room
Royal Academy of Arts
Mayfair, London, United Kingdom

1 December 2017

Théo de Luca *What comes to your mind when you hear about 'A New Spirit in Painting'?*

Tim Marlow It does seem like the moment when the Academy began to change. There was not a widespread exhibition culture at the time. The British Museum was doing major exhibitions, but the National Gallery was not; the Tate only did three exhibitions a year. Norman wanted to be more open and collegial with those institutions. The fact that he worked with Christos Joachimides – who was a friend of his in Germany, and the young Nicholas Serota – who was then at the Whitechapel, is significant to me. It is always seen as an exhibition authored by Norman, but he was collegial and he did work brilliantly with other people.

To work externally is an interesting model for the Academy. But also, the idea of moving into the territory of contemporary art, which is something the Academy tended not to do apart from the Annual Summer exhibition. Also, I think that there is now an orthodoxy of curated group shows. Every biennale seems to be a curated group show, every art fair seems to involve a variety of curated group shows. I am not against curated group shows or group shows per se, but 'A New Spirit in Painting' was genuinely original and felt like the beginning of a new kind of exhibition which sought to summarise the state of the art, or rather painting specifically in this case.

TdL *It is key to bear in mind that it was a group show. It is not an exhibition that changed the course of contemporary art but it is rather a vantage point on a specific moment in the history of painting. The exhibition gathered several streams, several trends, several painters trying to reflect on the idea of painting.*

TM In a very British context which also resonates internationally, the 1970s were a very contested decade regarding the status of the "art object". If you look at the history of British sculpture and that post-Kraussian idea of sculpture in the expanded field, there have been major controversies about what sculpture was and what it could be in the mid-1970s: the sculpture show at the Hayward, the acquisition of Carl Andre's works by the Tate... In the beginning of the 1980s, a whole generation of British sculptors emerged: Cragg, Woodrow, Deacon, Kapoor and others. Painting, on the contrary, was not seen as part of the late avant-garde mainstream. Anyway, this moment [the *new spirit*] was thought to be a "return to painting" but painting never went away. Painting has always had its place in the market. 'A New Spirit in Painting' was a reaffirmation of various European painting traditions, notably the Italian *Transavanguardia* and German Neo-Expressionism. Baselitz and Kiefer were exhibited one year after having represented Germany at the Venice Biennale. It is always seen as the emergence of that generation but the take on the older generation is more interesting: the acceptance of late Picasso changed, the reassimilation of Guston...

TdL *From a curatorial perspective, how challenging is it to bring to the same level works rooted in heterogeneous contexts?*

TM It is a very good question. 'A New Spirit in Painting' is not a model to follow but one of the problems is that it became so for some people. Its genius was to identify the moment when a disparate group of tendencies in painting seemed to come together, in a way that was meaningful because of the previous decade. It actually did try to identify a whole group of disparate tendencies, not just Neo-Expressionism. That was a strength. But there was a lot of disjunction in this exhibition too. It is extraordinary that Jasper Johns was not in it not to mention Agnes Martin. But the fact that the RA staged a major contemporary show had a major impact on the way the RA was viewed internationally too.

I think there are painting shows to do now. There could be an interesting show around history painting in contemporary art. But I think the idea of surveying the state of contemporary painting at the Royal Academy or anywhere else seems to be ill-advised or tedious today. It was of its time.

TdL *In what way was it of its time?*

TM Painting's status is no longer questioned but it was throughout the 1970s. 'A New Spirit in Painting' re-integrated painting into the more "serious" cultural discourses in the 1980s and beyond. Moreover, if you look at postmodernity, the fragmentation of forms and media, the globalisation of the art world, it was still permissible at the beginning of the 1980s to look at a Western tradition in a way that would be utterly reactionary now. In a sense, you could say it was a late opportunity for western modernism to re-examine itself. I think the other point is that artists such as Picasso (one of the last great masters in the sense of the "Old Master" tradition), de Kooning, Guston, Bacon, or Freud still had resonance and relevance alongside the emerging generation. That was the smartness of the curators to understand that.

TdL *Yes! The exhibition crystallised a certain state of things, rather than establishing a manifesto. Different tendencies were identified. If you look at the fate of the artists included in the show, you can today distinguish several heterogenous trajectories.*

TM Exactly! The pluralism that has been a dominant condition of art for the last three decades is also identified here...

TdL *Building on this idea of pluralism, what would you say about the relationships between painting and sculpture then? In the exhibition 'Zeitgeist' at the Martin-Gropius-Bau, Joseph Beuys's* Hirschdenkmäler *was displayed along with paintings. How would you interpret this shift from a show only including paintings to a show including paintings and sculptures? Is sculpture only something you bump into when you want to look at a painting?*

TM A very good question. I would stress the fact that at the Royal Academy, still in 2017, Academicians are elected in four categories. You're either a painter, a sculptor, a printmaker or an architect. That is quite a conservative way of breaking down what we call the fine arts. In the late 1960s and the 1970s, sculpture was, reductively speaking, seen as a more "advanced" art form. Krauss's notion of sculpture in the expanded field, the idea of post-minimal and Conceptual art... In sum, sculpture was much more porous: Gilbert & George were living sculptures, performance art was a form of sculpture... everything was an extension of a sculptural practice. Painting remained conservatively stuck on the canvas. My view is that the purity of the vision expressed through 'A New Spirit in Painting' was probably best conveyed in 'Zeitgeist'. Beuys's work is exemplary in this regard as it takes different directions. I would also say that Jasper Johns was including objects in his paintings from the 1960s and wasn't in the show. Picasso was as much a sculptor as he was a painter. Kiefer is as much as a sculptor as he is a painter. Baselitz is certainly a sculptor as well as a painter... and so it goes on. You find that the categories break down. On one level, throughout the 1980s, the re-emergence of painting was proclaimed. On another level, the blurring boundaries between painting and sculpture became much more marked. So, it's inevitable by this time: 1981, 1982... works were moving beyond the frame. Painting was under a similar process of deconstruction that sculpture had been through before. But it felt after-the-event. It felt unnatural because those arguments, those battles, those categories, those analyses had already happened. No one cared anymore about whether it was painting or sculpture... the status of the object had been unravelled and reconstructed. Art could go into all these territories. It was what the art was about or what it was doing rather than its own deconstruction that mattered.

TdL *If you think of the status of the exhibition within the Royal Academy's history, there is a gap between the controversy it provoked then and the way it is praised now. For instance, it is considered as the RA's seminal exhibition in the exhibition catalogue published for the Baselitz show in 2007.*

TM I think Norman knew it was a major statement and he intended it to be such. Actually, within the context of this institution, if Norman had left the Academy in 1983 and the Academy reverted to its more conservative exhibition programme, 'A New Spirit in Painting' would be more of a footnote in the history of Neo-Expressionist painting. But the fact that it really was a springboard for an extraordinary career here, and that Norman began to generate momentum around contemporary art… that made it doubly significant. I have a feeling that 'British Art in the Twentieth Century', 'Italian Art in the Twentieth Century', 'German Art in the Twentieth Century', 'American Art in the Twentieth Century' survey shows all came from the seeds down here [taps the exhibition catalogue]. This was done in less than eight months. So, the Academy was good at being lean and nimble.

TdL *It is as if the RA's agenda over the past few decades was announced through 'A New Spirit in Painting'. After 1981, the Italian, German, American and British Art in the Twentieth Century shows were organised, but also the Hockney shows in 1995, 2012 and 2016, Picasso in 1998, Guston in 2004, Baselitz in 2007…*

TM Kiefer! We all build a tradition. I think that until Anish Kapoor in 2010, there has not been a single main gallery-exhibition of a living artist. That was the last show curated by Norman. What I want to do with the Academy now is to work with some of the great living artists, in those spaces, making shows together, not surveying their careers, building on the idea of Kapoor, Hockney, Kiefer or Ai Weiwei… We build on that actually. You are absolutely right.
The critical response is to look at how great the works looked in those galleries. There is something about the quality of those spaces, how it works with contemporary art. There is something else which underpins this: a woman has never been given an entire main-gallery show. Marina Abramović will be there in 2020. She will be the first woman to be exhibited there. That's the thing that surprises me about 'A New Spirit in Painting': even in 1981, no woman artist was in the show. Alan Charlton rather than Agnes Martin, Susan Rothenberg should have been included too… I think that's another part of the legacy. Art was very male then and the RA was very much a

boys club with a few barely tolerated women members. That's all changed, thank god.

TdL *You have stressed that the show was done in less than eight months. The very essence of contemporary art is to be fugitive. The art world of today is not going to be the same in a year's time, whereas Tiziano is going to be basically the same next year...*

TM It is absolutely right! You survey a tendency. In a sense, 'A New Spirit in Painting' was already dated by the time it ended. The temporary nature of contemporary art is there. But to identify this tendency and to do it so quickly, within less than a year... all of that is the Academy's credit. That's also what made the selection quirky. All group shows take a speculative approach to what's interesting and what will be interesting in the future. The fact that it was done so quickly gave the show a sense of urgency and resonance. Some of the critics picked up on that. Even the reactionary ones, the ones who thought it was too fashionable.

TdL *You mentioned that there could be an interesting show around history painting in contemporary art. Do you think this idea of postwar history painting might be retrospectively one of the exhibition's Ariadne's threads? Much painters exhibited in 'A New Spirit in Painting' reflected on that genre. One could think of Anselm Kiefer's 'Operation Sea Lion' series (especially the painting from the Braman collection), or Cy Twombly's* Fifty Days at Iliam, *which is based on Homer's* Iliad *and is now part of the Philadelphia Museum of Art's collections. What's interesting is that history painting was much discussed and debated in nineteenth-century France, in the rise of modernity and modernism. The 1864 Salon was quite crucial in this regard: some of the critics encouraged painters to value history painting over landscape painting, reverting to the Académie's hierarchy of genres, Moreau's take on the story of Oedipus and the Sphinx went back to painters such as Ingres, David or Mantegna, Puvis de Chavannes took a different direction painting* L'Automne, *in which mannerist bodies merge with decorative elements, and so on.*

TM It's interesting you mention Kiefer because he always denies that he's a history painter in the conventional sense of the word, in the terms that Joshua Reynolds would have understood. But of course, history, as a grand subject as well as the specific events that take place in human past, is central to Kiefer's work. What I mean when I say 'an interesting show around history painting in contemporary art' isn't the continuation of the grand tradition of history painting. It's how in different places around the world, in the last fifty years, contemporary events and the recent past have been dealt with by art and painting specifically. So that would range from Warhol right up to a lof of contemporary Chinese painters. The framework would be vast. What makes it almost an impossible undertaking is that it would have to be global. So, how would you make that selection? But it's still an interesting provocation or idea. It goes back to the status of painting and the possibilities of painting. In a sense, there would be something conservative, even now, about a contemporary history painting show, because contemporary culture is dealt with by digital media, by film, by installation, by sculpture in the broader sense, very effectively, and perhaps more directly. But I think it's interesting to see how painting can re-examine its own possibilities. Given the status of history painting, the kind of pinnacle of Western painting from the fifteenth to the eighteenth centuries, that would be an interesting challenge to see how painting deals with that kind of subject matter in the recent past.

TdL *If one looks at the paintings brought together in 'A New Spirit in Painting', one could say that they do not deal with history painting in the conventional sense of the word but deal with history painting as a genre about the history of painting, which remediates the "Old Master" tradition in a fresh way.*

TM Painters have always referred to the art of the past, they do it in various ways. For example, Picasso had constantly referred to and deconstructed the "Old Master" tradition. From the 1950s onwards, he dealt with this more obviously and openly, re-examining his own position in relationship to that tradition, taking on quite literally "Old Master" icons from *Las Meninas* to *Le Déjeuner sur l'herbe* and so on. This tendency was not brand new but looking at the range of references which the painters from 'A New Spirit in Painting' embraced more explicitly is certainly interesting.

TdL *To conclude, I would like to go back to your remark on Jasper Johns. Which paintings would you have picked? Maybe Johns' crosshatchings would have been relevant – for example,* Scent *[1973-75] from the Ludwig Collection, or a painting similar to* Perilous Night *[1982] from the NGA. The former is embedded in the pictorial tradition and looks Cezannian while the latter echoes the art of quoting which underlies the history of painting.*

TM It would be much easier with the benefit of hindsight to say: 'these Jasper Johns' paintings might have been included.' You have mentioned *Perilous Night*, which of course was not finished as the show was being staged. That would have been interesting. Give me the benefit of hindsight: a fresh, large ambitious canvas by Jasper Johns, like *Perilous Night*, would have been fantastic.

Rainer Fetting
in conversation with Théo de Luca
Rainer Fetting's Studio
Neukölln, Berlin, Germany

10 January 2018
18 June 2019

Théo de Luca *How did you meet with Norman Rosenthal, Christos Joachimides and Nicholas Serota? How did you become involved in 'A New Spirit in Painting'?*

Rainer Fetting I have a few memories but I'm not sure how accurate they are. First, I knew Christos Joachimides because I was familiar with him already by the time of Moritzplatz. 'Selbsthilfe-Gallerie' was founded in 1977 and he was already familiar with Hödicke then. We had group shows at Moritzplatz... Lüpertz was very often at our openings. We partied with him, we all met in the Exil Restaurant. The owners are now the owners of the Paris Bar, and Christos was totally familiar with that scene. Then he met with Norman and they decided to do 'A New Spirit in Painting' in London.

TdL *Regarding your commitment to figurative painting, it was a statement at the time, wasn't it? Why did you choose to be involved in this kind of pictorial practice?*

RF It all happened step by step. So-called Berlin Realism, Conceptual art or Minimalism was nothing that turned me on. At the opposite of the art doctrines of the time, I intuitively saw a great and new chance in developing painting, which was kind of a taboo those days.

Joseph Beuys claimed that painting was dead, anachronistic. Everybody kind of followed those claims, even the artists who dared to paint. Immendorf erased his paintings by crossing them out demonstratively, and a generation of younger students set up on those beliefs.

Inspired by our shows on Moritzplatz – where painting became more and more important – and following the kind of carefree looking style of our paintings, reinvigorated with new subject matter, a whole new generation of painters suddenly showed up in West Germany, exaggerating our taboo-breaking painting concepts. Our fresh looking style became more than the talk of the town. While we enjoyed

every next piece of painting presented in our so-called "self-help gallerie", applauding with 'sehr gut', our success was also subject to hatred.
Nevertheless, a whole new generation of painters was pushed into the market simultaneously. This generation made sure that painting was kind of bullshit, but at the same time they promoted it.
Since Joseph Beuys had called painting 'dead', many artists believed that they had to be super ironical in order to apologise for their decision to paint.
But when the jokes were over, there was nothing left to paint.

TdL *But not all the painters you are listing were ironical, weren't they?*

RF In my eyes, it was more about ridiculing painting. But my interest was not in what they did.
I thought – following my own enthusiasm for painting and the paintings I saw and looked at in museums and so on – that "painting" in general has a huge potential, that would never end.
For example, my interest lied very much in the latest developments in painting, especially American Abstract Expressionism: Willem de Kooning, Mark Rothko, Jackson Pollock. I was also interested very much in their biographies, this is one reason why I moved to New York.

TdL *These were the artists you were looking at in the 1970s? De Kooning, Rothko…*

RF Even Andy Warhol. Especially the screen prints with underlying and hand-painted brushstrokes. I also liked how he dealt with his situation as an artist…

TdL *What drew your attention to Abstract Expressionist works?*

RF I must have seen a few paintings by de Kooning. I visited the Stedelijk Museum in Amsterdam. I saw his paintings but also his sculptures, the *Clamdiggers*. I saw his works that also connects to what was done before: the *Brücke* painters, German Expressionism... I was just interested in the way it was painted, the paintings were intense. I read biographies on de Kooning too. I really like his biography actually: he was an immigrant from Rotterdam; a clandestine passenger who travelled on a boat to America; how he integrated those art circles and met with those guys: Pollock, Rothko. It was very interesting to me from the mid-1970s.

In 1978, I was in New York and could see his works at the Museum of Modern Art. It was thrilling to be in the city where those painters used to work. I read every biography I could find – whether it was on de Kooning, Rothko or Pollock. I could never relate so much to the Germans who did abstract works after the war and decided not to paint figurative works anymore because of the Nazis. When I saw de Kooning and the other Abstract Expressionists, I wanted to do something similar but figurative, with the experience of having seen the huge formats they explored.

TdL *What about de Kooning's works included in 'A New Spirit in Painting'? Most of them are derived from Soutine's Céret paintings.*

RF Soutine was also important to me. I was interested in these flesh-like motifs, the weird perspectives he used. There is a feeling of *Taumel*. He was kind of an outsider. From his outsider-situation as a jew, he must have developed this outstanding painting style, which manifests itself as a unity of brushwork and iconography. This is what I see as the essence of painting. This tension I can figure out is also very strong in the painting of de Kooning for example.

TdL *Who were the other artists you looked at to keep on painting despite the context?*

RF Picasso was a great influence. I can see something from the way the works are painted. There is a whole history of this conception embedded in it. Velázquez is one of my favorite painters as well. You can still see how he paints. You can still see the brushwork. His paintings are like real, three

dimensional, you know. When I'm in the Prado, in front of a Velázquez, it's very abstract because you can see painting's structure, but at the same time it feels real, as if real people were breathing in front of you. That's something I want to do in my own time... to do something people can relate to, from their own experience of our society.
And why doing everything explicitly ironic?

TdL *What you've said about Velázquez reminds me of Alois Riegl's remarks in an essay he wrote in 1899,* 'Die Stimmung als Inhalte der modernen Kunst'. *For Riegl, modern artists extract* Stimmung *from artworks of the past and Velázquez is one of the artists he referred to. You can think of the* Rokeby Venus *from the National Gallery: all the details prove to be modern and seem to reveal why Manet called Velázquez "the painter's painter". Can you say more about your engagement with Velázquez's body of works?*

RF It might have something to do with how my father behaved in museums. He looked at every painting just the same way and wanted to get some information about the history of the paintings. I was first of all fascinated and attracted by the sensuality of a painting, something that jumps out at me because of the very way it is painted, not necessarily because of its historical background in the first place. My father just went from one painting to another in the same way and I was bored. Velázquez belongs to those painters I am drawn to. I can see that line from Velázquez to Manet. When I went to the Prado for the first time and saw *Las Meninas*, it looked as if the personal was alive. What strikes me in those paintings: I don't have to know about them, it's all about how they stand. When I went to art school there was Minimalism, Conceptual art, abstraction, *Berliner Realismus*... But I have always had painting on my mind.

TdL *When did you first go the Prado?*

RF I was travelling with Salomé. We started our journey in Holland. We then travelled all along the coast hitchhiking till Biarritz. From Biarritz we went to the Prado. That must have been around 1974.

TdL *Going back to this idea of sensuality, if you really look at Velázquez's paintings, figures are not drawn, it's rather made out of brushstrokes. If you look at each part of his paintings, you cannot tell whether it's an arm, a leg or a drapery. Is this a lesson you learnt from Velázquez? To really paint, you have to think pictorially and get rid of all the referential elements on your mind.*

RF Velázquez's paintings don't look perfect. I like his brushstrokes, which are amazing. Not everybody sees them. I first saw a Velázquez at the Prado and then I saw Goya. I have always thought that in Goya's paintings, there is too much caricature. The Velázquezs look as if they were breathing and stepping out of the canvas.

TdL *So you aim to achieve, say, something which is neither figuration nor abstraction, something that is embedded in a very fine research on technique...*

RF When I paint, I get results by digging and digging into the canvas. You have to get into a situation, where you let go more and more, and while you are digging in, you forget about your brain trying to be perfect. At the end of such an intense process, and seeing the painting again after a break you can see the result from a distance. From this point of reflection and surveillance, you have to work yourself into a trance again, and you are slowly working yourself through several processes forward in order to get hold of the painting. Seeing the different tracks of what you have done can give the painting that special tension. So it is not about producing refined techniques or about perfect looks.
Cézanne is very important that way and van Gogh of course. He was one of the main characters to point out this craving for the substance of what painting means.... Jackson Pollock was also doing it, but fighting representation, getting onto another ground.

TdL *You like the possibility to go beyond a simple relationship with* *the real so to say.*

RF The intuitive nature of painting, the way of searching for a kind of substance, that makes painting arousing and that tears you apart, that needs no explanations.

TdL *How do you paint?*

RF It's difficult to develop. It needs time. It looks sometimes spontaneous in the end. But the process can be sometimes very long. It can take weeks to develop a painting, but sometimes it comes out just like that.

TdL *What kind of materials do you use?*

RF I first started painting *a tempera* as a boy. In the 1970s, there was a shop near the wall where you could buy all the materials needed: cheap powder paint and so on. After earning good money, I have often changed. I worked with oil when I lived in New York. Recently, I have changed again because there are these huge formats… I often have to paint on the floor because I often prefer to paint very wet and very thin. So not to inhale all those tough liquids made of turpentine, I started painting with acrylics again, which are water-based.

TdL *You mentioned earlier the relationships between people and society. Society is indeed a recurring motif in your works, which sometimes challenge and question issues such as the representability of what happened during the Second World War.*

RF What's important to see is that, after the war, abstract painting was dominant. People considered that one could not paint figurative works anymore because of the Nazi painters. The Nazi painters made impossible to go on with figurative painting – this was the belief! But Nazi painting was kitsch because it was focused on Nazi ideology and was against the progression of art, against the so-called "*Moderne*".
But the Nazis have not created facts when they ruined figuration with their kitsch vocabulary… For me, it did

not mean that I had to stop painting figurative works in general! On the contrary! And who said painting is forever dead anyway?

TdL *What is your understanding of the "*Moderne*"?*

RF As far as I am informed about the term "*die Moderne*" in arts, referring to the history of art from the nineteenth and twentieth centuries, it means that artists are progressing with painting in their individual way and towards a new ground.
Important artists symbolising this attitude are, for example, Courbet, Cézanne, van Gogh or Picasso. A crucial impulse that initiated their drive to develop painting came from their discontent with "academic" styles. With their breakthroughs, they wanted to encourage the new and the fresh, not deadlocked styles and dogmas.
This thinking and way of seeing things are a major energy for the progression in arts. That is exactly what makes me feel the drive to paint.
It makes no difference if it already happened in the nineteenth or the twentieth century – "*die Moderne*", or even earlier – Velázquez, Goya, and so on. This very impulse throughout art history is the main drive in the development of painting up to these days.

TdL *How would you define the notion of "progress" in arts? Would it be something linear?*

RF I can't describe that. I don't think about it much. I use a lot of things that I see. Painting is under attack and is not taken seriously anymore because of the old techniques it uses. So what? You just take a brush and oil, go ahead and paint. I don't want to think about progress so much. In arts, I don't think something like that exists. It's like in music. I like Bach, for example. I am discovering more and more his organ works. I am not an expert of music history. But I personally don't like Wagner at all. I don't like to listen to the music of Beethoven either. Historians make a history up to Schönberg. I would not want to deny this line and it is not about personal tastes either. But for me, there's Bach and, nowadays, I consider Bob Dylan important, for example. My line of important music ranges from Bach to Bob Dylan, Hendrix, Blues, Jazz, Soul or Rap music.

TdL *What is your relationship with history as a painter? Do you use history as a subject matter?*

RF I already painted when I was as a child. My father was a teacher and often took me to museums. As I said, I thought his way of looking at paintings like a teacher was boring. I was more interested when I saw certain paintings that have that kind of sensitivity which arouses my interest.

TdL *So you are more interested in painting's expressive power rather than its ability to represent history or the now.*

RF These two things often happen hand in hand, especially after the war and because of all the things hidden and repressed by the population... It was nevertheless something that one could and should not ignore. The Nazi regime, the Holocaust... after the war, nobody really spoke about that in Germany. It took a long time. Germany was more interested in material things and prosperity than in its inner problems and its political division. But little by little, people worked on these issues. When I went to high school, the Nazi past was not a subject at all. From what I remember, some of the teachers must have been ex-Nazis themselves.

TdL *Did you want to deal with this subject in your paintings?*

RF Yes. The 'Shower' (*Große Dusche*) paintings, for example, were not only supposed to address the homosexual taboos of those days. It's also a mixture of all kinds of things that I wanted to combine.

I think I was one of the first painters to use figurative painting in order to work against this taboo of showing homosexuality in painting. In Germany, the paragraph 175 made homosexuality a taboo. Salomé and I were dealing with

these subjects. Salomé in an even more extreme or direct way. I remember that many collectors came and told me: 'Is this homosexuality you're dealing with? I don't care.' They pretended to ignore this aspect, underlining that they liked my paintings for their painterly qualities.
But when I painted those 'Shower' paintings, I also wanted to create an atmosphere that made people think unconsciously of the gas chambers in the concentration camps.
There are different versions of these 'Shower' (*Große Dusche*) paintings. I tried different expressions. One is now in the Erich Marx Collection (Figure 26), in the Hamburger Bahnhof, which is part of the Berlin National Gallery.

TdL *Was Moritzplatz a laboratory where you could combine your pictorial research with political issues?*

RF I don't know if Moritzplatz was this, because we all had different personalities, intentions and personal backgrounds. For all of us, it was a laboratory to deal with our own problems. We just formed that gallery so that we could exhibit our paintings that were neither shown nor accepted in other galleries.

TdL *How were your relationships with artists such as Baselitz or Lüpertz?*

RF I didn't even know Baselitz then, in the early 1970s, when I was in art school. I only knew certain galleries. Baselitz was not represented. I saw *Berliner Realismus*. But Lüpertz, Baselitz… I didn't see their works then.

TdL *When did you first see their works?*

RF It started when Hödicke applied for a professorship at my school. I became familiar with Hödicke's and Baselitz's works very late… But Hödicke was an influence from that moment on. Lüpertz too, especially his huge canvases. I was definitely influenced by that when I saw how he painted on big canvases with big brushes, something which I had done myself. But my own development was little inspired by their way of painting.

TdL *Did you know Penck?*

RF No...

TdL *Who was your professor?*

RF Professor Hans Jaenisch. He was a painter from the abstract generation, which came right after the war. He liked my paintings as soon as I had painted them. All the students in his class painted figuratively, in a free way – unlike in the foundation classes where we had to draw with sharp pencils. In the class next to mine, there were students who liked Beuys or Cy Twombly. To me, it seemed that they considered themselves as being more intellectual because too much explanations were necessary to understand their work.

TdL *Yet you were associated with Twombly in 'A New Spirit in Painting'.*

RF I think he belongs to a second generation of Abstract Expressionists. After Abstract Expressionism, the abstracts did not make much sense to me, or were not something I was interested in. Only Abstract Expressionists – such as Rothko, de Kooning and Pollock – drew my interest, since I also knew their biographies, as I have mentioned earlier.

TdL *Beuys's ideas had already reached Berlin from Düsseldorf at the time?*

RF Yes. He was a mainstream influence, and it seemed to me that, because he had to explain his work permanently, lecturing was more important than what the work did in itself. That was a boring thought to me.

TdL *Did you go to documenta in the 1970s?*

RF No, I have never been shown there. I was the only young painter from my generation included in 'A New Spirit in Painting', in London. Afterwards, other curators picked young new painters and promoted their work in every big art show taking place in West Germany.

TdL *What did you think of 'A New Spirit in Painting' when you first visited it?*

RF Of course, I was very proud. Suddenly, such a huge fame! To be shown with Picasso, Lucian Freud, Bacon, de Kooning and all the big painters. There was a lot of glamour then.

TdL *Did it bolster some of the ideas you had developed earlier?*

RF There were new fights under the art market's pressure, but all what happened then, good or bad, allowed me to live and work in New York. This triggered new things.

TdL *How was New York in the 1980s? Who were the people you met there?*

RF I somehow could put more effort into my own work then, which took enough energy. In 1983, when I moved there, graffiti was very hip, and I met artists like Daze or Richard Hambleton. Otherwise, I was not part of the glamorous scene, where artists like Sandro Chia, Francesco Clemente, Julian Schnabel or Keith Haring were being celebrated.

TdL *What about 'Zeitgeist' in 1982? Did it change Berlin? Was Berlin's status as one of the art world's hubs instigated by the show?*

RF Painting from Berlin was handled internationally then and my work was shown in international galleries in London, Zürich, New York and Paris.

TdL *How much did Berlin change after the fall of the wall, from an artistic point of view?*

RF From an artistic point of view or not, it was good because a lot of influences came in from outside. German thinking can be pretty monomaniac and lead to too much bureaucracy, which destroys creative thinking, flexibility and personal responsibilities. It leads to a state which is too demanding, to an attitude of expectation from others, that makes others responsible for their own mistakes. It makes people passive and phlegmatic. That's why new influences from outside are always good in order to initiate new thinking and energies.

Georg Baselitz
in conversation with Théo de Luca
Fondation Beyeler
Riehen/Basel, Switzerland

18 January 2018

Théo de Luca *If you look back today to the exhibition 'A New Spirit in Painting', how much does your work embody the* new spirit in painting? *Wenn Sie heute zurückblicken auf die Ausstellung 'A New Spirit in Painting', was würden sie sagen: in wie fern verkörpert Ihre Arbeit den neuen Geist der Malerei?*

Georg Baselitz The *new spirit* was a provocation and, in hindsight, an innovative provocation. Everyone was talking about the end of painting, and then there was this new beginning. Meanwhile, however, this exhibition is constantly being referred to and it has remained the most important exhibition to this day. Picasso was at the heart of it with his paintings, and everything else was around it. Physically, Picasso wasn't there, but he was there with his paintings. Der neue Geist war eine Provokation und rückblickend eine innovative Provokation. Man propagiert ja das Ende der Malerei und dann dieser neue Beginn. Inzwischen wird diese Ausstellung ständig zitiert und ist bis heute die wichtigste Ausstellung geblieben. Picasso stand mit seinen Bildern in der Mitte und alles andere war darum herum. Physisch war Picasso nicht da aber mit seinen Bildern anwesend.

TdL *And your own work in relation to that? Und Ihre eigene Arbeit in dem Zusammenhang?*

GB My own work was current and new, and I had the pleasure of hanging next to de Kooning. I was in an exceptionally lucky situation.
Meine eigene Arbeit war aktuell, neu und ich hatte das Vergnügen, neben de Kooning hängen zu dürfen. Ich hatte eine ausgenommen glückliche Situation.

TdL *In this context, would you think that your painting back then was future-oriented? In dem Zusammenhang würden Sie denken, dass auch Ihre eigene Malerei damals schon auf die Zukunft* *gerichtet war?*

GB That was never my idea. Futurism was never my idea. The past was always important to me. *Passatismo* or *Passato* – not as death, but alive, as a fount or source.
Das war nie meine Idee, Futurismus war nie meine Idee. Für mich war immer die Vergangenheit wichtig. *Passatismo* oder *Passato* – nicht als Tod, sondern lebendig, als Fundus.

TdL *Isn't your painting a painting for the future to some extent, because it reflects the quality of the medium and the history of the medium, so to speak? Ist nicht Ihre Malerei insofern eine Malerei für die Zukunft, weil sie quasi die Qualität des Mediums und die Geschichte des Mediums stark reflektiert?*

GB One thing is what the artist does, another thing is what happens to his pictures – in the evaluation, in the reflection of others, in the heads of others. I read a book about the *Neue Wilde*; I am considered the father, so to speak, or the first chapter. In any case, the book says I'm a dystopian painter. I didn't know the word and had to consult the dictionary.

When I was fourteen or fifteen years old, without any form of education, only with the idea in my head that I wanted to become an artist, I often went to the library. It was cleansed twice – once during the Nazi period and once again during communism. All art books with suspicious content were removed. I nevertheless found a book there from the 1920s called *Il Futurismo,* with black-and-white illustrations, intaglio prints by Boccioni and so on. So I see this book and these pictures for the first time, and had no idea about any of it before. I saw these pictures and thought – according to what it said on the front, *Il Futurismo* – that it was the future. Ten years ago, it became clear to me that this very future I had started with was already a thing of the past when I started. The people were dead and the pictures were a hundred years old.
Die eine Sache ist, was der Künstler tut, eine andere Sache ist, was mit seinen Bildern geschieht – in der Bewertung, in der

Reflexion der Anderen, im Kopf der Anderen. Ich habe ein Buch über die Neuen Wilden gelesen, da gelte ich sozusagen als der Vater, oder das erste Kapitel. Da stand drin, ich sei ohnehin ein dystopischer Maler. Ich kannte das Wort nicht und musste im Lexikon nachschauen.

Als ich vierzehn oder fünfzehn Jahre alt war, vollkommen ohne jegliche Bildung, nur mit der Idee im Kopf, Künstler werden zu wollen, habe ich sehr oft die Bibliothek besucht. Die wurde zweimal gesäubert, einmal während der Nazizeit und noch einmal während dem Kommunismus. Alle Kunstbücher mit verdächtigem Inhalt wurden entfernt. Ich fand dort trotzdem ein Buch aus den 20er Jahren das hieß *Il Futurismo,* mit schwarz-weiß Abbildungen, Tiefdruck von Boccioni und so weiter. Ich sehe dieses Buch und diese Bilder und hatte davon vorher keine Ahnung. Ich sah also diese Bilder und dachte, entsprechend dem, was da vorne draufstand *Il Futurismo,* das sei die Zukunft. Vor zehn Jahren wurde mir klar, dass diese Zukunft, mit der ich gestartet war, schon als ich startete, längst Vergangenheit war. Die Leute waren tot und die Bilder waren hundert Jahre alt.

TdL *I have two questions regarding the group Lüpertz, Kirkeby, Penck and Immendorf in the Michael Werner Gallery: would you say it was a 'laboratory' in the traditional sense of the word? And did the group have a common goal? Die Gruppe Lüpertz, Kirkeby Penck und Immendorf in der Galerie Michael Werner – da sind zwei Fragen dazu: Würden sie sagen, dass das ein Laboratorium im traditionellen Sinne war und würden Sie auch sagen, dass es ein gemeinsames Ziel dieser Gruppe gab?*

GB That was an emergency community. It was not the Black Mountain College and not the Bauhaus. There was a goal and that was to assert oneself. We had to assert ourselves.
Das war eine Notgemeinschaft. Es war nicht das Black Mountain College und nicht das Bauhaus. Es gab ein Ziel und das hieß, sich durchzusetzen. Wir mussten uns durchsetzen.

TdL *The next question is about the 1980 Venice Biennale. There* *is a quote by Harald Szeemann that the characteristic of the 1980 Biennale was that the production process remained visible in the finished works. Would you say that there is a correlation or an interaction of your body and your work within this process, in this physicality? Die nächste Frage dreht sich um die Biennale von Venedig 1980. Es gibt ein Zitat von Harald Szeemann, dass ein Charakteristikum dieser Biennale sei, dass der Herstellungsprozess in den fertigen Werken immer sehr stark sichtbar ist. Würden Sie sagen, dass es ein Zusammenspiel oder eine Wechselwirkung von Ihrem Körper und Ihren Werken in diesem Prozess, also diese Körperlichkeit, gibt?*

GB That can only be seen in context. Most of what was and what is are projections in whatever form – be it photos, videos or installations – for me, all of them are projections. I know this. And I know that it's always associated with modernity and I have always avoided being modern. I have always rejected this kind of representation for an artist. I believe and am firmly convinced that a pencil and a piece of paper are enough to deliver a document that enables everyone to recognise what is meant and what it is important. In my eyes, there is proof that it is wrong for an artist to design spaces if they want to be an artist in the traditional sense. I believe that a small surface or a large surface, a picture, is sufficient for an artist. Das kann man nur im Kontext sehen. Das Meiste was war und was ist, sind Projektionen, in welcher Art auch immer, seien es Fotos oder Videos oder Installation, ich nenne das alles Projektionen. Ich kenne das, ich weiß, dass das immer mit der Moderne in Verbindung gebracht wird und habe immer vermieden, modern zu sein. Ich habe diese Art von Darstellungsform für einen Künstler immer abgelehnt. Ich glaube, und ich bin fest davon überzeugt, dass ein Bleistift und ein Stück Papier genügen, um ein Dokument zu liefern, an dem jeder erkennt, was gemeint ist, und an dem jeder erkennt, dass es wichtig ist. Es hat sich für mich erwiesen, dass es für einen Künstler falsch ist, Räume zu gestalten, wenn er ein Künstler im traditionellen Sinne sein will. Ich glaube, dass eine kleine Fläche oder eine große Fläche, ein Bild, genug ist für einen Künstler.

TdL *Specifically regarding the conversation with Evelyn Weiss in 1975, you mentioned that you mostly work with your fingers. Is this about a bodily relation to the paintings or does working with your hands have to do with the* savoir-faire, *with the* métier, *with your handicraft? Nun spezifisch zu einer Unterhaltung mit Evelyn Weiss im Jahr 1975, wo Sie gesagt haben, Sie würden meistens mit den Fingern arbeiten. Die Anschlussfrage wäre, ob es um eine körperliche Beziehung zu den Gemälden geht oder ob Sie sagen würden, dass diese Art mit der Hand zu arbeiten eher mit dem* savoir-faire *oder mit dem* métier *oder mit ihrem Handwerk verbunden ist?*

GB Neither. The reason is that I always thought it was like playing golf but the other way around: you have to construct a handicap and use a crutch to overcome it. There is an artist I greatly appreciate who is long dead now. His name is [Ottone] Rosai, a Florentine who was very tall, unusually tall, taller than me, and who painted minuscule pictures. He made portraits of his friends the size of stamps. For this, he used his long arm and a long brush. That is how it is to be understood with the fingers. After all, the brush was invented as it is much more efficient.
Beides nicht. Der Grund ist, dass ich immer gedacht habe, wie beim Golf spielen, nur andersrum: Man muss ein Handicap konstruieren und muss eine Krücke benutzen, um dieses Handicap zu überwinden. Es gibt einen Künstler, den ich sehr geschätzt habe, der schon lange tot ist, er heißt Rosai, ein Florentiner, der sehr groß ist, ungewöhnlich groß, großer als ich, und der sehr kleine Bilder gemalt hat. Er hat Briefmarken große Portraits von seinen Freunden gemacht. Dafür hat er seinen langen Arm benutzt und einen langen Pinsel. So ist das auch zu verstehen mit den Fingern. Der Pinsel wurde ja erfunden, weil er viel effizienter ist.

TdL *Would you say that this has something to do with your stay at the Villa Romana in the 1960s? Würden Sie sagen, dass das auch mit dem Aufenthalt in der Villa Romana in den 1960er Jahren zusammenhängt?*

GB Finger painting has nothing to do with it. The stay in Florence was incredibly important and an unbelievably happy period, and I couldn't imagine my life without it. A scholarship made me financially secure for half a year. I got to know a culture and a past of which I had no idea and which deeply impressed me.
Die Fingermalerei hat damit gar nichts zu tun. Der Florentiner Aufenthalt war unglaublich wichtig und unglaublich glücklich und nicht wegzudenken aus meinem Leben. Ich war dort durch das Stipendium finanziell für ein halbes Jahr abgesichert. Ich habe dort eine Kultur kennengelernt und eine Vergangenheit, von der ich keine Ahnung hatte und die mich tief beeindruckt hat.

TdL *There are meanwhile many documentations of your working process – films and so on. Do you always paint quickly? How would you describe your working process? Es gibt ja mittlerweile sehr viele Dokumentationen Ihres Prozesses – Filme und so weiter. Malen Sie immer sehr schnell? Wie würden Sie ihren Arbeitsprozess beschreiben?*

GB In the meantime, I paint very fast. My start was tentative and I painted very slowly. I had big problems getting a picture done – with all this intent that I wanted to put into a picture. I have meanwhile become very professional and only need a few hours for a picture – not a day, a few hours, regardless of the format.
Inzwischen male ich sehr schnell. Ich habe sehr tastend, sehr langsam angefangen. Ich hatte große Probleme, ein Bild fertig zu bekommen, mit all dieser Absicht die ich in ein Bild hineintun wollte. Inzwischen bin ich sehr professionell geworden und brauche nur noch wenige Stunden für ein Bild – nicht einen Tag, wenige Stunden, unabhängig vom Format.

TdL *Let's talk about woodcuts and wood engravings, which is a German tradition. With the wood engravings that you work on, one could say that they have a certain power, a brutality. What does this power mean? Es geht um Holzschnitte und Holzstiche – das ist* *ja eine deutsche Tradition. Man kann ja schon beim Holzschnitt, wie Sie ihn bearbeiten, von einer gewissen Kraft, einer Brutalität sprechen. Was für eine Bedeutung hat diese kraft?*

GB Not brutality, but strength. If you have more strength, you can work more. But this has no real meaning. The strongest artist doesn't make the best woodcuts, but the most stupid makes the worst. But here's something more serious about woodcuts: I have always tried to do something contradictory. And at that time, when I started with making prints, there was offset, screen printing and so on. So I thought, great, you guys just all go ahead. But I will do something contradictory. I will do Burgkmair or Baldung Grien. Brutalität nicht, aber Kraft. Wenn man mehr Kraft hat, kann man mehr arbeiten. Aber eine wirkliche Bedeutung hat das nicht. Nicht der Stärkste macht die besten Holzschnitte, aber der Dümmste macht die schlechtesten. Noch was Ernstes zu den Holzschnitten: Ich habe immer versucht, etwas Widersprüchliches zu machen. Und zu dieser Zeit, als ich angefangen habe mit der Druckgrafik, gab es Offset, gab es Siebdruck und so weiter. Ich dachte wunderschön, macht ihr mal weiter. Ich aber mache etwas Widersprüchliches. Ich mache Burgkmair, ich mache Baldung Grien.

TdL *For you, is this also about being against what Pop Art stood for? Geht es Ihnen auch um ein dagegen sein für das wofür Pop Art stand?*

GB I thought Pop Art was great, really great, like a step on the moon. Another star has reached the moon. But there was no vocabulary in Pop Art that I could use. I am a great admirer of Pop Art and own several works by Andy Warhol, but we have nothing to do with each other except that he comes from Bohemia and I come from the Upper Saxony, and they are not far apart.
Ich fand die Pop Art großartig, wirklich großartig, wie ein Schritt auf dem Mond. Ein anderes Gestirn betritt den Mond. Aber es gab keine Vokabel in dieser Pop Art, die ich hätte verwenden könnte. Ich bin ein großer Verehrer der Pop

Art und besitze mehrere Werke von Andy Warhol, aber wir haben miteinander nichts zu tun, außer dass er aus Böhmen kommt und ich aus die Obersachsen und die sind sehr dicht zusammen.

TdL *Now let's talk about the subject. How important are European and Germany mythology in your work? Es geht jetzt ums Sujet. Wie wichtig sind europäische und deutsche Mythen im Werk?*

GB It is very important that I do not believe that angels exist north of the Alps. Angels are a mythological invention from the Mediterranean region that Christianity brought to us over the Alps. Although there is no justification for this here. Until Roman times, there were no angels north of the Alps – neither underground nor above ground. I always found it annoying to expect something that comes from above. For me, heaven and hell are completely unimaginable. One supposedly stands for hope and the other damnation. Accordingly, I worked with northern alpine, Germanic and Scandinavian myths. They came to me, just like for Richard Wagner and other Germans who revived these spirits of the past. My world is full of trolls and the like; in *The Lord of the Rings* they all have names like elves and dwarves and orcs. Dwarves are very important. Es ist wichtig, dass ich nicht akzeptiere, dass es nördlich der Alpen Engel geben soll. Engel sind ja eine mythologische Erfindung aus dem Mittelmeer Raum, die erst durch das Christentum über die Alpen zu uns gekommen sind. Obwohl es dafür bei uns hier gar keine Begründung gibt. Es gibt bis zur Römerzeit weder unterirdisch noch oberirdisch Engel nördlich der Alpen. Für mich war es immer irritierend, etwas zu erwarten das von oben kommt. Für mich sind Himmel und Hölle völlig unvorstellbar. Das eine soll ja Hoffnung und das Andere Verdammnis sein. Entsprechend habe ich nordalpine, germanische, skandinavische Mythen bemüht. Sie sind mir eingefallen, so wie es auch Richard Wagner und anderen Deutschen eingefallen ist, diese Geister der Vergangenheit wieder zu beleben. Also meine Welt sind Trolle und der Gleichen, in *Herr der Ringe* haben die alle Namen, also Elfen und Zwerge und Orks. Zwerge sind ganz wichtig.

TdL *In the* Physiologus *of Smyrna which you used, there is a strong contrast between text and image. To what extent is this interesting for you? My second question concerns the context of the eagle, which appears both in the* Physiologus *and your work: is that a pool or stock of material or how important is Christian symbolism, since you have hinted at that before? In dem* Physiologus *von Smyrna, den Sie verarbeitet haben, gibt es einen starken Kontrast zwischen Text und Bild. In wiefern ist das interessant für Sie? Und dann die zweite Frage wäre auch zu dem Kontext des Adlers, der im* Physiologus *vorkommt und bei Ihnen vorkommt. Ist das eher ein Fundus von Material oder wie wichtig ist auch da die christliche Symbolik, da haben Sie ja schon mal ein bisschen angedeutet?*

GB The *Physiologus*, my *Physiologus*, is that of Smyrna who was burned in the Greco-Turkish War, and which only exists as a photocopy. But that was not why I created *Malelade.* I started *Malelade* and asked myself: what is it that you want to do here? Then I remembered the farmer's calendar, the folk calendar, the *Physiologus*; I looked in the library and found out that I was on the right track. Then I made this strange children's book, in this children's language, which is actually more Hölderlin than Gottfried Benn. And I think that because I did everything myself, the verses, the writing, the drawing, that it has become quite interesting. Der *Physiologus*, mein *Physiologus* ist der von Smyrna der im türkisch griechischen Krieg verbrannt worden ist, den es nur als Photokopie gibt. Das war aber nicht der Anlass Malelade zu machen. Ich habe *Malelade* angefangen und habe mich gefragt: Was ist das, was du hier machen willst? Dann fiel mir der Bauernkalender, der Volkskalender, der Physiologus ein, ich habe in der Bibliothek gesucht und habe festgestellt, dass ich auf dem richtigen Weg bin. Ich habe dann dieses eigenartige Kinderbuch gemacht, in dieser Kindersprache, das eigentlich mehr Hölderlin ist als Gottfried Benn. Und denke, weil ich alles selbst gemacht habe, die Verse, die Schrift, die Zeichnung, dass das ziemlich interessant geworden ist.

TdL *Regarding the exhibition of Fraktur-Bildern in 1982 at Anthony d'Offay's, "Ruins: Strategies of Destruction in the Fracture*

Paintings of Georg Baselitz, 1966–69'. There is a substantial narration about the aesthetic of ruins – for example, the destruction of the Bastille, and the ruin as a symbol for something historic but also for chance. In your work, one could see the body as a ruin or as a modern monument: is that something that is close to you? Es geht um die Ausstellung der Fraktur-Bildern 1982 bei Antony d'Offay, "Ruins: Strategies of Destruction in the Fracture Paintings of Georg Baselitz 1966–69'. Es gibt eine große Narration über die Ästhetik der Ruinen, zum Beispiel der Zerstörung der Bastille und die Ruine als Symbol für etwas Historisches aber auch für Zufälligkeit. Und bei Ihnen könnte man den Körper als Ruine sehen oder als modernes Monument – ist das etwas das Ihnen Nahe liegt?

GB Well, I didn't line up as a figurative painter the likes of Auerbach, Freud or Bacon. For me, the representational world came to an end in 1958 with Pollock's exhibition in Berlin. My painted world until 1969 was an invented world, a world of myths, a world of monsters, a world completely out of touch with reality. Until 1969, I had always jumped against the bars of a cage. With the inversion, I suddenly took a step that made me completely independent of the real world, in which I could use it in a very peculiar way – namely, turn it upside down. Also, ich bin ja nicht angetreten als gegenständlicher Mahler wie Auerbach, Freud oder Bacon. Für mich ist die gegenständliche Welt 1958 mit der Ausstellung von Pollock in Berlin zu Ende gegangen. Meine gemalte Welt bis 1969 war eine erfundene Welt, eine Mythenwelt, eine Monsterwelt, eine ganz realitätsfremde Welt. Bis 1969 bin ich immer gegen Käfigwände gesprungen. Mit der Umkehrung habe ich dann plötzlich einen Schritt gemacht, der mich ganz unabhängig von der wirklichen Welt gemacht hat, in dem ich sie auf eine ganz eigenartige Weise verwenden konnte, nämlich auf dem Kopf.

TdL *Time and time again, it is claimed that the upside-down paintings are also an ironic reaction to Beuys's claim that 'painting is dead'. Would you say it was an ironic reaction? And was it only ironic? Es wird immer wieder behauptet, dass die Gemälde auf dem Kopf eine Reaktion auf Beuys: „Die Malerei ist tot", zu lesen sind.*

War das eine ironische Reaktion oder nur eine ironische Reaktion?

GB I never heard Beuys proclaim that painting was dead. But that was already said when I was a student. The Nouveaux Réalistes said, 'panel painting is dead'. I thought to myself, well, then, it has died, but I will still paint because what else am I supposed to do: I paint as an avant-gardist, not as a reactionary. And it wasn't difficult at all because there were no pictures on the left and right. On my first visit to London, I was confronted with a different kind of painting – by Bacon, Freud, Auerbach and Kossoff – which was realistic in a way, but also very natural and good, and which was not possible in our cultural circle. Then I thought about what had actually happened there. I was lucky enough to find a way out mentally. I said to myself that these artists had taken a leap in time, that they had emigrated to England as children, and that when they began to express themselves artistically, they expressed themselves in the past that they had left behind – in other words, in 'Berlin Realism'. And for me that was actually the intellectual basis, the certainty that the doctrine stating 'the picture is dead' was complete nonsense. Ich habe nie gehört, dass Beuys gesagt habe, dass die Malerei tot sei. Aber das wurde schon gesagt als ich Student war. Die Nouveaux Réalistes sagten, „das Tafelbild ist tot". Ich dachte mir ja gut, dann ist es gestorben, aber ich male trotzdem, denn was soll ich sonst machen, ich male dann eben als Avantgardist, nicht als reaktionär. Das war auch gar nicht schwer, denn es gab ja links und rechts auch keine Bilder. Bei meinem ersten Besuch in London wurde ich mit einer anderen Malerei konfrontiert – von Bacon, Freud, Auerbach und Kossoff, die in einer Art und Weise realistisch, aber auch sehr selbstverständlich und gut war, die in unserem Kulturzirkel gar nicht möglich ist. Dann habe ich darüber nachgedacht, was dort eigentlich passiert war. Ich hatte dann das Glück, gedanklich einen Ausweg zu finden. Ich sagte mir, diese Künstler haben einen Zeitsprung gemacht, die sind als Kinder nach England emigriert, und als sie angefangen haben, sich bildnerisch zu äußern, haben sie sich in der Vergangenheit geäußert, die sie verlassen hatten, sprich im

Berliner Realismus. Und das eigentlich war für mich die intellektuelle Basis, die Sicherheit, dass die Doktrin, „das Bild ist tot" ein völliger Unsinn war.

TdL *Would you say that sculptures are an extension or embodiment of painting? Würden Sie sagen, dass die Skulpturen Erweiterung oder Verkörperung der Malerei sind?*

GB I would say that sculpture and painting have little in common. Precisely what I do with paintings is not possible with sculptures. Sculptures are like ghosts. Whatever you want, whether you hang them from the ceiling or put them on the floor, they always somehow remain ghosts. Ich würde sagen, Skulptur und Malerei haben wenig miteinander zu tun. Genau dass was ich bei den Bildern machen, ist bei Skulpturen nicht möglich. Skulpturen sind wie Geister. Wie man auch will, ob man sie an die Decke hängt, oder auf den Boden stellt, sie sind immer rgendwie Geister.

TdL *In 1979, you said that every work of art is created in the head of the artist and also stays in the head of the artist. The question is how you decide on what medium these ideas in your head will be realised – if it is going to be either painting or sculpture? Sie haben gesagt, 1979, jedes Kunstwerk entsteht im Kopf des Künstlers und bleibt auch im Kopf des Künstlers. Die Frage wäre wie entscheiden Sie diese Ideen, die in Ihrem Kopf sind? In welchem Medium realisieren Sie sie? Eher als Malerei oder Skulptur?*

GB I held a lecture back then called 'The Painter's Equipment' (1985) and I started with cave painting, with catacomb painting. This was done by painters without any chance that the painting would ever come to light. And that's how it stayed. It was only 2,000 years later that these paintings came to light. The idea that a picture never comes to light is very fascinating. This means that the painting remains in the painter's head; although they have executed it, nobody can see it. This I find very interesting as an intellectual retreat. Ich habe damals einen Vortrag gehalten, der hieß das „Das

Rüstzeug der Maler“ (1985) und ich bin von der Höhlenmalerei, von der Katakombenmalerei ausgegangen. Diese wurde von Malern gemacht, ohne Chance, dass das Bild jemals ans Tageslicht kommt. So ist es auch geblieben. Erst 2.000 Jahre später kamen diese Malereien ans Tageslicht. Dass ein Bild niemals ans Tageslicht kommt, ist eine sehr faszinierende Idee. Das heißt noch weitergetrieben, das Bild bleibt im Kopf des Malers, er hat es zwar ausgeführt, aber niemand sieht es. Und ich finde das als intellektuellen Rückzug sehr interessant.

TdL *Would that make the paintings incomplete because there is still something left in the head? Würde das im Umkehrsinn Ihre eigenen Bilder unvollständig machen, weil immer noch etwas im Kopf bleibt?*

GB There is not one picture in my work, there is not one catacomb, but there are sixty years of pictures, and there are actually many fragments that fit together like a puzzle. Es gibt nicht ein Bild bei mir, es gibt nicht eine Katakombe, sondern es gibt sechzig Jahre Bilder und eigentlich gibt es viele Fragmente, die sich zusammenfügen, wie ein Puzzle.

TdL *That would be the next question: has your work also become real, in the sense of a cosmos, a whole, and not only as a number of series? One generally likes to divide into series. Dann wäre die weitere Frage ob Ihr Werk dann tatsächlich auch real als Werk im Sinne eines Kosmos, eines Ganzen, gesehen werden muss und nicht als eine Anzahl an Serien. Man teilt ja so gerne in Serien ein.*

GB It has surprisingly become a cosmos – I would never have believed this.
I always thought that I was simply making a section and then a new section, and that both sections didn't fit together. I thought they were radical breaks. But if you look at it from today's perspective, you can see that it's a cosmos.
Überraschender Weise ist es, was ich nie geglaubt habe, wirklich ein Kosmos geworden.

Ich dachte immer, ich mache einen Abschnitt und danach einen neuen Abschnitt, und beide Abschnitte fügen sich nicht zusammen. Ich dachte, es seien radikale Brüche. Aber wenn man es von heute aus betrachtet, dann sieht man, dass es ein Kosmos ist.

Jean-Louis Froment in conversation with Théo de Luca Hôtel Bourg Tibourg Marais (4th arrondissement), Paris, France

12 February 2018

Théo de Luca *A geography of the history of painting of the 1970s can be unfolded from the exhibition 'A New Spirit in Painting'. The CAPC must be associated with it. What was your position, the one of the CAPC, in the debates at that time? À partir de l'exposition 'A New Spirit in Painting', il est possible d'établir une géographie de l'histoire de la peinture des années soixante-dix. Le CAPC doit y être associé. Quelle était votre position, celle du CAPC, dans les débats de l'époque ?*

Jean-Louis Froment 'A New Spirit in Painting' and 'Zeitgeist' were art manifestos, rather than exhibitions; two cultural encounters which revisited the fundamental archetypes of European painting, in the context of the predominance of American art, which was totally hegemonic.
In these exhibitions, the works presented revealed the origins of European culture and established ties with the universality of the myths which have built that very culture.
After the American victory and its consequences, European art finally attempted to recreate itself and to appear artistically.

I had already become aware of this approach, through my meetings with Julian Schnabel, whom I had met early on in New York by the end of the 1970s. His painting questioned European classics already.
Later on, in 1980, there was an exhibition on Anselm Kiefer at the Venice Biennale, to which the CAPC was invited to present its activities through the exhibition 'Esperienza a Bordeaux'.
The exhibition on Anselm Kiefer clearly expressed a thought whose roots – whether they were cultural, historical, mythical or philosophical – were European.
That was a disturbing exposure of Germany's ashes; what was repressed by a whole generation.
It opened a breach in the memory of the untold and the painters grasped what surfaced.
I felt that I had to bring this new debate in Bordeaux and

make it resonate beneath the vaults of the CAPC.

In Venice, I contacted Kiefer to put on an exhibition of his works in 1984 – the moment when the CAPC was refurbished and acquired the status of museum, simultaneously with an exhibition on Cy Twombly – we can never place enough emphasis upon the importance that Cy Twombly, an American who chose Italy as a place to live and to work, had on those painters' generation.
'A New Spirit in Painting' et 'Zeitgeist' ont été des manifestes artistiques, bien plus que des expositions ; deux rencontres culturelles qui revisitaient les archétypes fondamentaux de la peinture européenne, dans un contexte de prédominance artistique américaine, carrément hégémonique.
Dans ces expositions les œuvres présentées révélaient les fondements d'une culture européenne et tissaient un lien avec l'universalité des mythes qui l'ont construite.
Après la victoire américaine et ses conséquences, l'Europe artistique tentait, enfin, de se reconstituer et d'apparaître artistiquement.

J'étais déjà sensibilisé à cette approche, au cours de mes rencontres avec Julian Schnabel, dont j'avais fait la connaissance très tôt à New York à la fin des années soixante-dix. Sa peinture interrogeait déjà les classiques européens.
Un peu plus tard, en 1980, il y a eu cette exposition d'Anselm Kiefer à la Biennale de Venise, où le CAPC était invité à présenter ses activités à travers l'exposition 'Esperienza à Bordeaux'.
L'exposition d'Anselm Kiefer exprimait clairement une pensée dont les racines – culturelles, historiques, mythiques, philosophiques – étaient européennes.
C'était une mise en vue dérangeante des cendres de l'Allemagne ; le refoulé d'une génération.
Une brèche s'ouvrait dans la mémoire des non-dits et ce qui est apparu a été saisi par les peintres.
J'ai bien senti qu'il fallait que j'amène ce nouveau débat à Bordeaux et le faire résonner sous les voûtes du CAPC.

À Venise, j'ai donc pris contact avec Kiefer, pour une exposition de ses œuvres en 1984 – date de l'espace réaménagé et ouverture du CAPC avec le statut de Musée, simultanément à la présentation de l'exposition de Cy Twombly – on n'insistera jamais assez sur l'importance que Cy Twombly, américain ayant choisi l'Italie comme lieu de vie et de travail, a eu sur la génération de ces peintres.

TdL *In the exhibition catalogue of the 1980 Venice Biennale, Szeemann wrote quite a crucial remark. For him, a new artistic phase was beginning and would be characterised by a research on a new formal alphabet, which would involve the body and make visible the artistic process, through forms and materials. Dans le catalogue d'exposition de la Biennale de Venise de 1980, Szeemann écrit une remarque assez cruciale. Pour lui, une nouvelle phase artistique s'était récemment ouverte et se serait caractérisée par la recherche d'un nouvel alphabet formel, qui engagerait le corps et laisserait visible le processus artistique, à travers les formes et la matière.*

JLF The involvement of the body can also be found in the work of Mondrian and Ryman.
A painting naturally represents the body of the person who painted it. A body does not require a visible (even agitated) pictorial gesture to be represented in a painting. It can also exist through restraint and discretion.
The gaze can perceive this.
Do you think the body is not visible in a monochrome by Yves Klein ?
It is true that we witnessed the insertion of culture-specific materials into the works of that time: Arte povera was part of Kiefer's painting, Gaudi's broken ceramics were part of Julian Schnabel's painting… as many European references.
There was especially – with the emergence of figuration which had deserted exhibition spaces (but not the artists' studios) for several decades for the benefit of abstraction – a new iconography, a new look on history, on universal myths.
Once again, one should look toward Cy Twombly.
L'engagement du corps on le trouve aussi chez Mondrian et

chez Ryman.
Une peinture représente naturellement le corps de celui qui la peint. Un corps n'a pas besoin d'un geste pictural visible (voire agité) pour se représenter dans une peinture. Il peut exister également par sa retenue, sa discrétion.
Le regard est capable de déceler cela.
Pensez-vous que le corps n'est pas visible dans un monochrome d'Yves Klein ?
Il est vrai qu'on a pu assister dans les œuvres de cette époque à l'introduction de matériaux culturellement identifiés : l'Arte Povera est entré dans la peinture de Kiefer, les céramiques brisées de Gaudi dans la peinture de Julian Schnabel... autant de références européennes.
Il y avait surtout, avec l'arrivée de la figuration, qui avait déserté les lieux d'exposition (mais pas les ateliers des artistes) depuis quelques décennies au profit de l'abstraction, une nouvelle iconographie, un regard sur l'histoire, sur les mythes universels.
Encore une fois, il faut regarder vers Cy Twombly.

TdL *With regard to that question of history, it seems that certain artists included in 'A New Spirit' questioned the representability of the Second World War and attempted to dialogue with that period. This recalls the preoccupations of Paul Celan, who raised the question 'What poetry after Auschwitz?' As for us, we can formulate similar questions. What painting after Auschwitz? What plastic formulations to explore? Are these questions you asked yourself? À propos de cette question d'histoire, il semble que certains artistes du 'New Spirit' ont interrogé la représentatibilité de la Seconde Guerre mondiale et essayé d'entrer en dialogue avec cette période. Cela rappelle les préoccupations de Paul Celan, qui souleva la question 'Quelle poésie après Auschwitz ?' À notre tour, nous pouvons formuler des interrogations semblables. Quelle peinture après Auschwitz ? Quelles formulations plastiques explorer ? Est-ce que ce sont des questions que vous vous êtes posées ?*

JLF Why make this notion of history still?
I think that life's power renews, as it absorbs memory, this notion of history and goes beyond Paul Celan's famous phrase.

I will quote one which is just as painful, fatalistic but nonetheless *perpetual*:

'A nothing
we were, are, shall
remain, flowering:
the nothing-, the
no one's rose.'

[Ein Nichts
waren wir, sind wir, werden
wir bleiben, blühend :
die Nichts-, die
Niemandsrose.]

At that moment everything stopped and nothing stopped in the world; in different places for each and every one of us.
I think of the painting of Baselitz, who dealt with Germany's collective memory with a singular power and boldness.
His pictorial vocabulary signifies the representation of the subjects he addresses: to cut, to mutilate the figure, to introduce the khaki colour used for German uniforms... to turn the logic of the gaze upside down and thus invert our perception. To disrupt the logical order of thought.

In the exhibition 'Légendes', in 1984 at the CAPC, there was a gallery composed of a selection of paintings by Baselitz from the 1960s and of the portraits of famous Jewish people painted by Warhol.
The portrait of Kafka was placed between two pictures by Baselitz.
At the same time as the exhibition 'Légendes', there was an exhibition on Kiefer's paintings in the grand nave of the CAPC and, in the ground floor galleries, there was an exhibition on Cy Twombly.
Here is my answer to Paul Celan's question.
Pourquoi rendre immobile cette notion d'histoire ?
Je pense que la puissance motrice de la vie renouvelle, tout en absorbant la mémoire, cette notion d'histoire et dépasse cette

célèbre phrase de Paul Celan.
Je citerai celle-ci, tout aussi douloureuse, fataliste mais néanmoins *continuelle.*

« Un rien
nous étions, nous sommes, nous
resterons, en fleur :
la rose de rien, de
Personne. »

À ce moment-là tout s'est arrêté dans le monde et rien ne s'est arrêté ; à des endroits différents pour chacun d'entre nous.
Je pense à la peinture de Baselitz, qui a traité de la mémoire de l'Allemagne avec une force et une audace particulières.
Son vocabulaire pictural est signifiant de la représentation des sujets qu'il aborde : sectionner, mutiler la figure, introduire le vert kaki des uniformes allemands… renverser la logique du regard et donc inverser notre perception. Bouleverser l'ordre logique de la pensée.

Dans l'exposition 'Légendes', en 1984 au CAPC, il y avait une salle composée par un choix de peintures des années soixante de Baselitz et les portraits des juifs célèbres peints par Warhol. Le portrait de Kafka par Warhol était placé entre deux tableaux de Baselitz.
En même temps que cette exposition 'Légendes', il y avait l'exposition des peintures de Kiefer dans la grand nef et, dans les salles du rez-de-chaussée, une exposition de Cy Twombly.
Voici ma réponse à la question de Paul Celan.

TdL *In the exhibition 'Légendes', you also exhibited Fautrier. If one had to establish a genealogy, he would be associated with Baselitz. The* 'Otages' *series is quite pertinent in this regard. In 1945, in the catalogue of the exhibition organised by the Galerie Drouin, Malraux asked a question about it, 'Aren't we uncomfortable with those almost gentle roses and greens which seem to belong to Fautrier's indulgence in another part of himself.' Dans l'exposition 'Légendes', vous exposez aussi Fautrier. S'il y avait une généalogie à établir, il serait associé à Baselitz. La série des* 'Otages' *est assez* *pertinente à cet égard. En 1945, dans le catalogue de l'exposition organisée par la Galerie Drouin, Malraux pose une question à son propos, 'Ne sommes-nous pas gênés par ces roses et verts presque tendres qui semblent appartenir à une complaisance de Fautrier pour une autre part de lui-même ?'*

JLF The tragic power of Fautrier's paintings – I remember seeing certain pictures by Fautrier at Baselitz's in Derneburg and their presence opened up the door to a perspective on the work of Baselitz – certainly lies in those colours which are for me the colours of absence, the colours of the shreds of tragedy.
The power of an artwork is the power of the multiplicity of the interpretations about it.
Which works were placed along Fautrier's paintings in the exhibition 'Légendes'?
La force dramatique des peintures-déchirures de Fautrier – je me souviens avoir vu certains tableaux de Fautrier chez Baselitz à Derneburg et leur présence m'a ouvert une perspective sur l'œuvre de Baselitz – tient certainement de ces couleurs qui pour moi seraient celles de l'absence, celles des lambeaux du drame…
La force d'une œuvre d'art est la force de la multiplicité de ses interprétations.
Quelles œuvres étaient placées avec les tableaux de Fautrier dans l'exposition 'Légendes' ?

TdL *Baselitz's and Kounellis's sculptures. Des sculptures de Baselitz et de Kounellis.*

JLF It was in 1984.
The tragedies of today's world are even more visible; what would be the dialectics of such an exhibition today?
Maybe I would like to undertake this task.
Which artistic dialectics?
Which selection of works?
C'était en 1984.
Aujourd'hui, les drames du monde actuel sont encore plus visibles ; quelle serait la dialectique d'une telle exposition ?
Voici un exercice auquel j'aimerais me livrer peut-être.

Quelle dialectique artistique ?
Quel choix d'oeuvres ?

TdL *Kiefer has engaged with Germanic culture. One could say that he created gap phenomena in the 1970s, via the collage of heterogeneous iconographies.*
The 'Heroisches Sinnbild' *series depicts Nazi figures in the midst of romantic landscapes and alongside mythologizing German sculptures from the eighteenth and the nineteenth centuries. For example, August Wredow's* Iris Takes the Fallen Hero to Olympus. *Kiefer thus seems to archive Nazism in German culture. It also seems that his gestuality is more penetrating and acid than other artists included in 'A New Spirit', like Malcolm Morley, who employs gentle colours and sensual bodies. Kiefer s'est emparé de la culture germanique. On pourrait dire qu'il a créé des phénomènes d'écart dans les années soixante-dix, via le collage d'iconographies hétérogènes.*
La série 'Heroisches Sinnbild' dépeint des figures nazis au sein de paysages romantiques et aux côtés de sculptures allemandes mythologisantes des XVIIIe et XIXe siècles. Par exemple, Iris portant le héros tombé à l'Olympe *d'August Wredow. Kiefer semble ainsi archiver le nazisme dans la culture allemande. Il semble aussi que sa gestualité est plus pénétrante et acide que d'autres artistes du 'New Spirit', comme Malcolm Morley, qui a recours à des couleurs douces et des corps sensuels.*

JLF He is both the heir of Joseph Beuys and Caspar David Friedrich.
Kiefer managed to capture the symbolical eloquence of history (not only German history) and to use signifying materials – how not to think of lead, zinc, fire – to inscribe the often disturbing and unsettling signs of the culture of his origins into his painting.
This culture is also ours.
He always seeks a close relationship between his gesture, the material and the subject he deals with; which gives to his works a strong intensity.
There is a battle.
In Kiefer's paintings, the pictorial material is predominant

compared with the subject.
It assaults our thought before we understand what we are dealing with.
The material from sunflowers strikes us before we remember van Gogh!
In the scenes he paints, Morley favours representation. The gesture, the active pictorial expenditure, are (visibly) less important.
Il est à la fois l'héritier de Joseph Beuys et de Caspar David Friedrich.
Kiefer a su capter la force d'évocation symbolique de l'histoire (pas seulement allemande) et utiliser des matériaux signifiants – comment ne pas penser au plomb, au zinc, au feu – pour inscrire dans sa peinture les signes souvent troublants et dérangeants de la culture de ses origines.
Cette culture est aussi la nôtre.
Il cherche toujours une relation étroite entre le geste, la matière et le sujet qu'il traite ; ce qui donne à ses oeuvres cette forte intensité.
Il y a un combat.
Dans les tableaux de Kiefer, la matière picturale est prédominante par rapport au sujet.
Elle assaille notre pensée avant que l'on comprenne de quoi il s'agit.
La matière des tournesols nous saisit avant que nous retrouvions van Gogh !
Morley peint des scènes dont il privilégie la représentation. Le geste, la dépense picturale active, sont (visiblement) moins importants.

TdL *Going back to the opposition between Europe and the United States, which you outlined through the figure of Julian Schnabel, 'A New Spirit in Painting' was an exhibition formulated against New York's hegemony. Was establishing yourself in Bordeaux a means to inflect or to dislocate the art world's geography? Pour revenir à l'opposition entre l'Europe et les États-Unis, que vous avez esquissée à travers Julian Schnabel, 'A New Spirit in Painting' est une exposition formulée contre l'hégémonie de New York. Est-ce que s'établir à Bordeaux a été une façon d'infléchir ou de disloquer* *la géographie du monde de l'art ?*

JLF It had been built up progressively with more intuition than determinism.
Between 1973 and 1983, the CAPC had been fluctuating, nomadic, uncertain about its perenniality. The status of museum gave this perenniality to the CAPC in 1984.
Through those exhibitions (and the whole activity of the CAPC), it was about taking a stance from France in the context of a cultural debate that went way beyond the art world.
I always thought of the CAPC as a tool.
I showed Baselitz before Kiefer showing first his drawings in 1980, in the exhibition 'Baselitz, Beuys, Penck'. Then, I showed his sculptures in 1983, for the first time in France.
I was really impressed by Baselitz. Ileana Sonnabend and I traversed East Germany to visit him in his castle in Derneburg, where I discovered, among other things, his collection of Primitive Art.
A world in contradiction with the idea of modernity that I had.
Tout s'est construit progressivement avec plus d'intuition que de déterminisme.
Entre 1973 et 1983, le CAPC était flottant, nomade, incertain de sa pérennité. Le statut de musée la lui a donné en 1984.
À travers ces expositions (et l'ensemble des activités du CAPC), c'était prendre position depuis la France dans un débat culturel qui dépassait le seul monde de l'art.
J'ai toujours pensé le CAPC comme un outil.
J'ai montré Baselitz avant Kiefer en commençant par exposer tous ses dessins en 1980, dans l'exposition 'Baselitz, Beuys, Penck'. J'ai ensuite montré ses sculptures en 1983, pour la première fois en France.
J'étais très impressionné par Baselitz. Nous avons traversé, avec Ileana Sonnabend, l'Allemagne de l'Est pour aller lui rendre visite dans son château à Derneburg, où j'ai découvert, entre autres, sa collection d'art primitif.
Un monde qui s'opposait à l'idée que j'avais de la modernité.

TdL *What was your idea of modernity then? Quelle était votre idée de la modernité à cette époque-là?*

JLF The one of a young man in his thirties, who thought about what was surface in the world in which I was evolving; without any real meditation but with a lot of worries.
Actually, this absurd notion of 'contemporary' certainly blurred my relationship with the world.
The beauty and the meaning of the word '*inactual*' definitely embraced me and definitely resolved my relationship with time.
Celle d'un jeune homme de trente ans, qui pensait à ce qui était en surface du regard dans le monde dans lequel j'évoluais ; sans beaucoup d'approfondissement mais avec beaucoup d'inquiétude.
En fait cette notion absurde de « contemporain » flouait certainement mon rapport au monde.
La beauté et le sens du mot « *inactuel* » m'a définitivement rejoint et a définitivement réglé mon rapport au temps.

TdL *Bearing in mind this idea of modernity, you associate Barthes with Baselitz and further artists from his generation in 'Légendes'. Barthes wrote, 'my own historical position is to be at the rear-guard of the avant-garde: to be avant-garde one must know what is dead; to be rear-guard, one must still love it.' En gardant à l'esprit cette idée de la modernité, vous associez Barthes avec Baselitz et d'autres artistes de sa génération dans 'Légendes'. Barthes a écrit, « ma propre position historique est d'être à l'arrière-garde de l'avant-garde, être d'avant-garde c'est savoir ce qui est mort, être d'arrière-garde c'est l'aimer encore. »*

JLF The 'historical' position of Barthes remains his; delicate and rhetorical. A beautiful semantic pirouette which can help us reflect on our own position.

In this exhibition, Barthes was *amicably* indispensable.
With Henri Michaux, more than writing, they both questioned 'the written form', this primitive state of the trace and this temptation to trace the unreadable like an unconscious state of reading.
And the frame of this exhibition: Dubuffet, Michaux, Fautrier, these postwar artists were present too.

More than a question of modernity, of 'rear- or avant-garde', which refer to sectarian historicist notions, it would be the '*inactual*' feeling of this exhibition which made it interesting.
La position « historique » de Barthes demeure la sienne ; sensible et rhétorique. Une belle pirouette sémantique qui peut nous aider à réfléchir sur notre propre position.
Dans cette exposition, Barthes était *amicalement* indispensable. À proximité d'Henri Michaux, plus que l'écriture, à eux deux ils interrogeaient « la graphie », cet état primitif de la trace et cette tentation de tracer l'illisible comme un geste inconscient de lecture.
Et puis le cadre de cette exposition : Dubuffet, Michaux, Fautrier, ces artistes de l'après-guerre étaient aussi présents.
Plus qu'une question de modernité, « d'avant ou d'arrière-garde » qui renvoient à des notions historicistes sectaires, ce serait le sentiment « *inactuel* » de cette exposition qui en faisait son intérêt.

TdL *The exhibitions you did show it: they are intertwinements of photographs, texts, artworks, drafts... a bit like* Roland Barthes by Roland Barthes. *The development of the CAPC coincides with the emergence of a new form of what one clumsily calls the "curator".*
In this context, how did you reflect on the nature of your activity? What was your way of putting on exhibitions? How did you work?
Les expositions que vous avez faites en témoignent : elles sont des entrelacements de photos, de textes, d'œuvres d'art, de brouillons... un peu comme Roland Barthes par Roland Barthes. *Le développement du CAPC coïncide avec l'apparition d'une nouvelle forme de ce que l'on appelle maladroitement le "commissaire d'exposition".*
Dans ce contexte, comment réfléchissiez-vous sur la nature de votre activité ? À quoi ressemblait la façon dont vous construisiez des expositions ? Comment travailliez-vous ?

JLF We are a bit far from the topic of this conversation and I have to say I look backward with a lot of difficulties.
I have always said '*I write a museum*'. Of course, it is a metaphor which insists on the endeavour that I undertook to make

the whole readable for both the artists and the visitors. I wrote this museum, from the architecture to the exhibitions programmes, from the department of education to the library.
I was not a director or a curator.
I was a writer.
Nous sommes un peu loin du sujet de cet entretien et j'avoue que j'ai beaucoup de difficultés à regarder en arrière.
J'ai toujours dit « *j'écris un musée* ». C'est bien sûr une métaphore qui insiste sur l'application que j'ai pu apporter à rendre l'ensemble lisible autant pour les artistes que pour les visiteurs. J'ai écrit ce musée, de l'architecture aux programmes des expositions, du service éducatif à la bibliothèque.
Je n'étais pas directeur ou commissaire.
Je suis un auteur.

TdL *That's what I thought looking at the CAPC's history, which spans from 1973 to 1996: one can clearly see the construction of a real thought-space, a* Denkraum. *C'est ce que j'ai pensé en regardant l'histoire du CAPC, de 1973 à 1996 : on peut clairement voir la construction d'un véritable espace de pensée, d'un* Denkraum.

JLF It is the artworks which give these dimensions.
Art is thought, isn't it?
Ce sont les œuvres qui donnent ces dimensions.
L'art c'est de la pensée, n'est-ce pas ?

TdL *In the film produced for the Louvre's exhibition titled 'Treatise on the Line', Damisch said that exhibitions allow for any sort of connection. Dans le film produit pour l'exposition du Louvre nommée 'Traité du trait', Damisch dit que l'exposition autorise toute sorte de rapprochement.*

JLF History is suffocating. Its application on museums even more.
Today, the young generation took a considerable distance from the museum's historicist task multiplying the points of view, working on exhibitions-fictions, engaging with their personal history.
Art can also be a material of interpretation, its wealth is

paradoxical, this way of slipping into diverse temporalities, which is unique.
I like the handicraft proper to the construction of an exhibition, which echoes writing.
I think of certain exhibitions I put on and which were shown in other museums: I took the same vocabulary and something else told itself.
The power of art is that very thing: the multiplicity of entrances. This is the problem of writing, one can say opposite things with the same words.
The practice of poetic writing and the practice of the writing of an exhibition fall under the same method.
L'histoire est étouffante. Son application muséale encore plus. Aujourd'hui, la jeune génération a pris une distance considérable par rapport à l'exercice historiciste du musée en multipliant les points de vue, en travaillant des expositions-fictions, en engageant son histoire personnelle.
L'art peut être aussi un matériau d'interprétation, sa richesse est paradoxale, cette façon de se glisser dans des temporalités diverses, unique.
J'aime cet artisanat de la construction d'une exposition qui évoque l'écriture.
Je pense à certaines expositions que j'ai montées et qui ont été montrées dans d'autres musées : je prenais le même vocabulaire et autre chose se racontait.
La force de l'art c'est cela même : la multiplicité des entrées. C'est le problème de l'écriture, on peut dire des choses opposées avec les mêmes mots.
La pratique de l'écriture poétique et la pratique de l'écriture d'une exposition relèvent pour moi d'une méthode identique.

TdL *A saying by Cassirer states that the poet is an alchemist who transforms language into gold. Une formule de Cassirer dit que le poète est un alchimiste qui transforme le langage en or.*

JLF Thinking that the same word can keep people alive and kill them.
The same language creates the dullest texts and the most beautiful poems.

Art is dangerous.
Penser qu'un même mot peut faire vivre des gens et les faire tuer.
La même langue crée les textes les plus insignifiants et crée les poèmes les plus beaux.
C'est dangereux l'art.

TdL *Building on this idea of the CAPC as a thought-space, I am particularly interested by the exhibition catalogues. They form a collection. The essays published in them show high standards of theoretical insights, which seem to be lost today: Hubert Damisch for 'Art Minimal II', Philippe Sollers for 'Légendes', Marcelin Pleynet for 'Simon Hantaï 1960-1976', Giovanni Careri on Kounellis for 'Peinture. Emblèmes et Références' and so on. One could also quote the conferences of Derrida, Szeemann, Damisch or Buchloh, the archives of 'Art Minimal I & II', which nurtured the writing of* Ce qui nous voyons, ce qui nous regarde *by Georges Didi-Huberman. To what extent did your exhibitions produce theory? Toujours dans l'idée du CAPC comme espace de pensée, les catalogues d'exposition m'intéressent particulièrement. Ils forment une collection. Les essais qui y sont publiés témoignent souvent d'une haute exigence théorique, qui semble aujourd'hui perdue : Hubert Damisch pour 'Art Minimal II', Philippe Sollers pour 'Légendes', Marcelin Pleynet pour 'Simon Hantaï 1960-1976', Giovanni Careri sur Kounellis pour 'Peinture. Emblèmes et Références' et ainsi de suite. On pourrait aussi citer les conférences de Derrida, Szeemann, Damisch ou Buchloh, les archives d''Art Minimal I & II', qui ont nourri l'écriture de* Ce qui nous voyons, ce qui nous regarde *de Georges Didi-Huberman. Dans quelle mesure pensez-vous que vos expositions ont été productrices de théorie ?*

JLF The word *theory* rather reflects the dominant spirit of the end of the 1960s.
And one has often confused '*theorising on art*' with '*reflecting on art*'. There are often trendy terms which loose their meaning as they are overused.

The philosophers, the writers the CAPC welcomed had overcome that sectarianism.

One did not deal much with the poetic but the power of poetry was infiltrating everywhere; naturally.
You mention Marcelin Pleynet who is a poet and wrote beautiful texts on art.
Personally I do not want to oppose the two against each other.
An exhibition must allow for the emergence of a point of view that is particular, theoretical, poetic, or other things, an assemblage of ideas which can be contradictory. The power of an artwork lies in the depth of the interpretations that can be derived from it.
The exhibition must seize it and work on this postulate.
Le mot *théorie* reproduit davantage l'esprit dominant de la fin des années soixante.
Et puis on a souvent confondu « *théoriser sur l'art* » et « *réfléchir sur l'art* ». Il y a souvent des termes tendances qui perdent leur sens par excès d'utilisation.

Les philosophes, les écrivains que le CAPC accueillait avaient dépassé ce sectarisme.
On ne touchait pas trop au poétique mais la force de la poésie s'infiltrait partout ; naturellement.
Vous évoquez Marcelin Pleynet qui est un poète et qui a écrit de beaux textes sur l'art.
Personnellement je n'ai pas envie d'opposer les deux.
Je pense qu'une exposition doit faire émerger un point de vue particulier, théorique, poétique, ou autre, un ensemble d'idées et pourquoi pas contradictoires. La force d'une œuvre d'art est dans l'étendue des interprétations que l'on peut en faire.
L'exposition doit s'en saisir et travailler ce postulat.

TdL *It is also fruitful to look at the CAPC's programme at that time. You were not orthodox or a hard-liner. You did not solely show one type of artists or works. You also presented Minimal art and Conceptual art in the 1980s. You wanted disputes, you wanted to provoke debate. Il est également fécond de regarder le programme du CAPC à cette époque-là. Vous n'avez pas été orthodoxe ou jusqu'au-boutiste. Vous n'avez pas montré qu'un seul type d'artistes ou d'œuvres. Vous avez également présenté l'art minimal et l'art conceptuel dans les années 1980. Vous vouliez de la dispute,* *provoquer des débats.*

JLF I thought that it was important to bring one thing and its opposite, so that the public could react to what it was about to see and to what it had seen, so that it could ask itself questions and understand that there is not solely a single way of making art – that would be authoritatively mandatory (the one of history, for example), in order to discover the meaning of an artwork in an exhibition.
It was entirely deliberate. The ruptures were sometimes strong. However, we always felt loyalty to key artists, often opposed in their approaches, in their thoughts.
I think that it is the artists who made this place.

The public had several rendezvous with the same artists as much as the artists had multiple rendezvous with the CAPC.
It was magic. For example, Gilbert & George participated in the sensitive construction of the CAPC: exhibitions, performances…
Mario Merz, Lawrence Weiner, Laurie Anderson, Daniel Buren or Richard Long *'lived'* in the place. The museum was a welcoming land for artists. The public met with them. It was shared. The staff of the museum took care of the artists. Beyond the place, links have been established between the city, its inhabitants and the artists.
Je pensais qu'il était important d'amener une chose et son contraire, pour que le public réagisse à ce qu'il allait voir et à ce qu'il avait vu, qu'il se pose des questions et comprenne qu'il n'y a pas qu'une seule voie – celle qui serait autoritairement obligatoire (celle de l'histoire, par exemple), pour découvrir le sens d'une œuvre d'art dans l'exposition.
C'était totalement délibéré. Les ruptures étaient parfois fortes. En revanche, il y a toujours eu une fidélité à des artistes clés, souvent opposés dans leurs démarches, dans leurs pensées.
Je pense que ce sont les artistes qui ont fait ce lieu.

Le public a eu plusieurs rendez-vous avec les mêmes artistes tout autant que ces artistes ont eu de multiples rendez-vous avec le CAPC.

C'était magique. Par exemple, Gilbert & George ont beaucoup participé à la construction sensible du CAPC : expositions, performances…
Mario Merz, Lawrence Weiner, Laurie Anderson, Daniel Buren ou Richard Long ont « *habité* » le lieu. Le musée était ce territoire d'accueil pour les artistes. Le public les rencontrait. C'était partagé. Le personnel du musée prenait en charge les artistes. Au-delà du lieu, des liens se sont créés entre la ville, ses habitants et les artistes.

TdL *What are your unrealised projects at the CAPC? Quels sont vos projets non-réalisés au CAPC ?*

JLF I renounced three projects for identical circumstances. There was a project with Beuys and another with Warhol. These exhibitions did not take place because both artists passed away. I thought it was interesting to invite Warhol in the grand space to make a wallpaper project.
Beuys, who was interested by the CAPC, wanted to make a site-specific project, in the grand space. One no longer speaks about Beuys today… it is curious. For my generation, Beuys was decisive.
The third project – which could still happen today (since the concept is still in the museum's archives and has been awaiting completion for twenty-five years) with Félix González-Torres – did not take place for the same reasons.
J'ai renoncé à trois projets pour des circonstances identiques. Il y a eu un projet avec Beuys et un autre avec Warhol. Ces expositions n'ont pas eu lieu parce qu'ils sont décédés. J'avais trouvé intéressant d'inviter Warhol dans le grand espace pour y faire un projet de papier peint.
Beuys, qui était intéressé par le CAPC, voulait faire un projet spécifique, dans le grand espace. On ne parle plus de Beuys maintenant… c'est curieux. Pour ma génération, Beuys était déterminant.
Le troisième projet, qui pourrait encore se faire (car le concept est encore dans les archives du musée en attente de réalisation depuis vingt-cinq ans) avec Félix González-Torres, n'a pas eu lieu pour les mêmes raisons.

TdL *For a part of the so-called "figurative" painters from the 1970s, Beuys was an enemy to be vanquished. In which way, was he decisive for your generation? Pour une partie des peintres dits « figuratifs » des années soixante-dix, Beuys était un ennemi à abattre. De quelle manière, était-il déterminant pour votre génération ?*

JLF Formally, yes.
A way of shaping a biographical thought that could nonetheless have a universal resonance, particularly through his performances, the poverty of his representations, the abandon of a narrative figuration that had become academic, a work, an artistic approach, which resist you, the integration of the living in art... life as a material...
Formellement, oui.
Une manière de mettre en forme une pensée biographique qui pouvait néanmoins avoir une résonance universelle, particulièrement à travers ses performances, la pauvreté de ses représentations, l'abandon d'une figuration narrative devenue académique, une œuvre, une approche artistique qui vous résistent, l'engagement du vivant dans l'art... la vie comme matériau...

TdL *To conclude, what would you say about museums and artistic creation today? Pour conclure, que diriez-vous des musées et de la création artistique aujourd'hui ?*

JLF It is the works which strike me, displace my thoughts, activate my knowledge, arouse my anger or my serenity, give me a full measure of the world. Their venues, patterned after a world sold to the highest bidder, are to be reinvented.
As soon as I erased the word '*contemporary*' from my vocabulary, the word '*art*' has been cleaned up from all the toxic temporalities.
I have looked elsewhere.
Ce sont les œuvres qui m'interpellent, déplacent mes pensées, activent mes connaissances, éveillent ma colère ou ma sérénité, me donnent une mesure du monde. Leurs lieux d'accueil, à l'image d'un monde vendu aux plus offrants, sont à réinventer.

Sitôt que j'ai effacé le mot « *contemporain* » de mon vocabulaire, le mot « *art* » s'est trouvé débarbouillé de toutes les temporalités toxiques.
J'ai regardé ailleurs.

Anthony d'Offay
in conversation with Théo de Luca
Mayfair, London, UK

15 October 2019
17 October 2019

Théo de Luca *What was the state of art at the beginning of the eighties? How did it influence your decision to expand your gallery in London?*

Anthony d'Offay 1979 was a very important moment: Joseph Beuys had a major retrospective at the Guggenheim Museum in New York, and the world of contemporary art seemed to change. It was the whole museum, from top to bottom. Thomas Messer, director of the Guggenheim, thought he was going to be fired for taking out a window of the iconic Frank Lloyd Wright building in order to install *Tallow* [1977], Beuys's sculpture consisting of twenty-two tons of fat.

I remember very clearly the private view at the Guggenheim, with Beuys standing in front of the gallery up the first curve, on his own. As people walked upstairs, including important American artists such as Bruce Nauman and Lawrence Weiner, Beuys kissed them on the lips, which was surprising, shocking and beautiful.

The work that was in the exhibition was unlike anything in American art or anything that American art knew at this time. Immediately, when you saw the show, you felt that you had to rethink contemporary art. How did you take on board this strange-looking person, strange-acting person who did this extraordinary art? This was a whole new way of presenting ideas and putting them in context. It had nothing to do with art for art's sake, but everything to do with understanding the world we live in. Beuys was completely unlike anyone else.

I mention all of this, because I believe Beuys – and his New York retrospective in particular – are part of the context for 'A New Spirit in Painting'. It was as though he opened a door, and out came a new generation of non-American young artists.

We opened our new gallery in 1980 with Joseph Beuys's big room installation, *Stripes from the House of the Shaman*, which was acquired from us by the National Gallery of Australia in Canberra.

TdL *Although Joseph Beuys was seen as a controversial figure by many artists from 'A New Spirit in Painting', he was arguably still a teacher and source of inspiration to many others. In this respect, 'Zeitgeist' was and still is an influential exhibition insofar as Beuys exhibited with the American, German and Italian painters. Interestingly enough, you did an exhibition of Beuys' drawings in 1981: 'Words Which Can Hear'. What did Beuys think of the revival of the idea of painting?*

AdO Beuys had several lives. He had an intense life teaching young people. When you were with him, he could speak and explain things beautifully. He liked the idea that suddenly he was in a room with a hundred people and three blackboards. He also had a life in the Green Party, of which he was a co-founder. One of his most famous works is *7,000 Oak Trees*, in the city of Kassel. That looks like a work perhaps for our time, or a moment still to come. He was somebody who was looking at an entirely new way of making art: he was not looking at art history and judging it. I was in New York two or three weeks ago and there were the Beuys trees with those basalt stones beside them, growing on 22nd Street. You can imagine that *7,000 Oak Trees* was quite a shocking thing at the time, although it seems prescient considering the state of the environment today. That is what this artist did. He was not thinking about the renewal of painting.

However, when he came to London, as he did whenever he was installing a show with us, he had all his meals in this room. We would make sure to have interesting people there: Nicholas Serota, David Sylvester and other artists. I remember Cy Twombly was in town and we invited him to come and meet Beuys. There was an extraordinary dialogue between them in which each spoke of the passion he felt when looking at the work of the other.

TdL *Today, at the Kunsthaus Zürich, there is a room in which Beuys's* Olivestone *is paired with Twombly's* The Vengeance of Achilles. *They had a dialogue in your gallery and now it continues through their work. Which artists did you discover in 'A New Spirit in Painting'?*

AdO I was very moved by the paintings of Willem de Kooning. I was lucky enough to become a friend of his and of his New York dealer, Xavier Fourcade. Then I started visiting de Kooning and spending the afternoon in his studio with him. We did two important exhibitions in 1984 and 1986, and sold a lot of pictures to museums around the world.
It was a wonderful experience being with him. He was small and still had a strong Dutch accent. He did not talk much. He just liked to be quiet with the paintings and let them speak to him. Whenever I left, he came outside and would bow and say, 'give my love to London.' It meant a lot to him that he was having an exhibition in a great capital city and that his work would be seen there. He was a genius. If you look at his works and his chronology, you can see that the 1960s were in some way overshadowed by the 1950s. Without a doubt, he returned to greatness in 1975 when he began a new cycle of paintings, including *...Whose Name Was Writ in Water*, a work which haunts me still.

TdL *In the text David Sylvester wrote for the exhibition organised by the NGA in Washington, DC, he recounted his visits to de Kooning's studio in Springs, by East Hampton, which is, according to him, akin to Holland. De Kooning moved to the other side of the Atlantic Ocean and found the same atmosphere. Can you recount how de Kooning painted?*

AdO There would be probably eight or twelve paintings that he would be working on. It was important for him to look at each of them intensely in silence. Occasionally, he would go up and put a brushstroke on a painting. Mostly, he was just thinking and being with the paintings.
De Kooning was interested in being able to say something that was true, universal and had not been said before. If you look at his works from the 1950s, they are great paintings. Suddenly, he began to paint these women. I do not think he intended to paint women at all. I think they came and said to him, 'this is what you have to do.' He was obeying the truth as he saw it.

TdL *Which artists included in 'A New Spirit in Painting' would you* *have liked to show?*

AdO Bacon, Guston, Balthus, Hockney. If you look after Bacon, for example, that is a full-time job for five people. We looked after some great artists, but I am not sure Bacon would have liked all the artists that we were showing. It was thrilling when I first came to London and was able to see a new show of Francis Bacon at Marlborough Gallery. It was also very exciting in London when Hockney was a young artist showing with John Kasmin.

TdL *You got to know Bacon through Lucian Freud. Did you ever go to Bacon's studio at 7 Reece Mews?*

AdO I never went to Reece Mews. I felt loyal to Lucian. I did not want, perhaps, to think that Bacon was a better painter than Lucian. Lucian was the greatest painter of his time, of his date. One of the wonderful things that Francis Bacon did was to look after Lucian like a member of his own family.
We did two extraordinary things for Lucian's career. One was when we presented a beautiful exhibition of Lucian's paintings in 1971. David Sylvester saw it and thought that the paintings were terrific. Then, he went to the Arts Council and suggested they do a big exhibition. So, Lucian had a major show with the Arts Council, which changed how people regarded him. He was no longer Francis's little friend who painted nice pictures. He became a major British painter.
The other thing that happened came in 1988, when we did an exhibition of Leigh Bowery in performance at our gallery. He was a big and outrageous Australian performance artist who also worked with the dancer and choreographer Michael Clark. Leigh did an intense week of extraordinary performances at our gallery in Dering Street. Leigh created an entirely new persona – and costume to match – each day, and, accompanied by an otherworldly soundtrack of insects, would adopt various poses through a one-way mirror, so only the audience could see him. Lucian came every day and when they met Leigh became an important part of Lucian's life. Leigh's personality and physical presence inspired Lucian to

paint giant canvases of Leigh naked. These pictures became a radical turning point for Lucian, and the beginning of a new exhibition cycle with the prestigious Acquavella Gallery in New York in 1992, followed by the Metropolitan Museum in 1993.

TdL *How were the "new names" – such as Baselitz, Kiefer or Richter – received by Lucian Freud?*

AdO I never talked to him about those things. They just seem like very different worlds, and I left it like that.

TdL *You also collaborated with Warhol. When did you begin to work with him?*

AdO In 1981. I already knew Andy, and we immediately had a discussion about having a show in London. He told me, 'come back and tell me what you want to do, then we will talk about it and I will do it.' It was an enormous responsibility. I said to him, 'let's work on a great new self-portrait.' He said, 'I will take photographs and then we will look at them together and choose the image.' I went to New York and there were indeed dozens of images. He pointed out one which he liked, but I said, 'Andy, it has something of a death mask.' I pointed out another which was similar, but without the feeling of death – we agreed to make an exhibition with this image.
Just as I was leaving, he said, 'I'd like to make some with camouflage.' My heart sank, and I asked him perhaps to do one camouflage self-portrait so that we could look at it together. Three weeks later, the camouflage painting was hanging opposite the desk of Brigid Berlin on the ground floor of the Factory. It was a masterpiece, and I felt ashamed not to have trusted the artist completely.
In 2008 we gave to the Tate Gallery the best *camouflage* painting Andy ever made, *Camouflage*, a four-panel masterpiece from 1986 – one of more than 100 paintings and drawings in the ARTIST ROOMS collection.

TdL *What about the relationship between Beuys and Warhol?*

AdO Beuys, like Warhol, was a real star. People would always recognise him and start to gather around, sometimes forming a big crowd. Beuys was a star and this very fabled person, just as Andy was. There was nobody else like Beuys in Europe. He was a genius. He was involved in politics, in education and so on. Same for Andy. They loved and admired each other because they could see that each of them could create this sort of world, that they were both very different stars, that they both dealt with the world in a different way.

When I first met with Beuys, he asked me what I wanted him to do, like Andy in a way, so I bought a book and asked him to do some drawings in it. When Andy was being interviewed, he would say the worst possible things imaginable. For instance, when people asked, 'why did you come to London?' He would reply, 'oh, I kinda ran out of money.' When people asked, 'why did you do self-portraits?' He would reply, 'I guess I kinda ran out of ideas.' That was a big thing of Andy's, to act simple and innocent. When we did projects with him, you could really tell him what to do. So, we always avoided the question of whether the works would be a commercial success, and concentrated on what would be important for Andy and art history. Above all, what we wanted was for Andy to do something important, beautiful and iconic.

TdL *Which countries and cities were strategically important in the 1970s and the 1980s to promote painting? Did the art world's geography change around 1981? This period seems to be a time when it was possible to put on culturally ground-breaking exhibitions in cities that would be regarded as provincial today – the CAPC in Bordeaux might be a quintessential example.*

AdO It was just a few people who believed very strongly in putting on great shows: Nicholas Serota, for example, as well as Norman Rosenthal, Rudi Fuchs, Harald Szeemann and Christos Joachimides. It really came down to these people and the exhibitions they did. It was a message which also got carried by Jean-Louis Froment in Bordeaux: that art has its own power.

TdL *When it comes to Beuys and 'A New Spirit in Painting', one of the artists one can immediately think of is Anselm Kiefer.*

AdO Anselm spoke about the few precious days that he had spent with Joseph Beuys in his studio as the most important time in his life. I visited Beuys every month and each day was a treasured experience, so I can well believe the strength of Anselm's memories. We did some extraordinarily beautiful shows with Kiefer, and gave many important works of his to Tate and the National Galleries of Scotland.

Of course, Nick Serota did a magnificent exhibition of Anselm's at the Whitechapel Gallery. It was marvellous in every way and a great introduction to the shows we organised shortly after in our gallery.

I was in Kiefer's studio one day. He had a plan chest. I asked what was in it and pulled out a drawer. It was filled with important early watercolours. Immediately, I promised Anselm to work on the collection, and to bring it to the Metropolitan Museum of Art, where it remains to this day.

Nicholas Serota in conversation with Théo de Luca Brown's Hotel Mayfair, London, UK

16 October 2019

Théo de Luca *What comes to your mind when you reflect on 'A New Spirit in Painting'?*

Nicholas Serota One of the interesting things about 'A New Spirit in Painting' is that when people talk about it now, they talk almost exclusively about the shock and surprise provoked by the inclusion of the expressive German painters – Baselitz, Penck, Kiefer, Lüpertz, artists whose work was not really well known in England and America, or even recognised within the art market. However, at the time people were also surprised by the inclusion of the much older generation of artists: on the one hand, Picasso, Hélion, Matta and Balthus, on the other, de Kooning, Bacon and Guston. People tend to forget that Robert Ryman and Brice Marden were also included in the exhibition. So it rather had at least three strands to it. It probably slightly diluted the message of the exhibition. When Norman and Christos did their 'Zeitgeist' exhibition in Berlin the following year, there was a clearer message because they abandoned the more minimal artists and the older generation.

The commitment to 'A New Spirit in Painting' was made very late by the Royal Academy. Which exhibition was cancelled?

TdL *The exhibition on the masterpieces from the Gemäldegalerie Alte Meister Kassel.*

NS Norman was invited to make a proposal for an exhibition of contemporary art which would not need the long lead time required for an historical exhibition with loans from public and private collections. Initially, he had a discussion with Christos. They felt that it would be helpful if I was involved in the exhibition because I had close contact with certain artists and I would add a slightly different dimension. I had worked with Christos on an exhibition at the Whitechapel in 1978, a show about artists working in Berlin titled '13° East: Eleven Artists Working in Berlin'. What interested me was that Christos was someone with a very wide range of reference. Later, he became associated largely with this generation of painters, but at the time, he was closely engaged with Beuys and a number of artists whose work had a strong social message. For me, from a British point of view, he had a very interesting European sensibility, coming originally from Greece, working for a long time in Berlin. His view of the world was very different from a British or American view. I had been interested in what was happening in Germany. In parallel with working with him on '13° East', I was also making a Richter exhibition which was shown at the Whitechapel in 1979, the first substantial Richter exhibition in Britain.

TdL *Under your directorship, the Whitechapel prepared the ground for 'A New Spirit in Painting'. As you said, you did the exhibition '13° East' with Christos. It's also interesting that later on you were to do solo shows on several artists who exhibited in 'A New Spirit in Painting': Guston, Baselitz, Kiefer, Schnabel, Twombly, Hodgkin and so on. What about the message behind 'A New Spirit in Painting' did you want to convey to a British audience? Did it have anything to do with Britain in particular or was it more directed at a global stage?*

NS I think the exhibition was very much directed at a global audience. I thought that it would also set the scene for the programme that I wanted to do at the Whitechapel and that if it succeeded in addressing a global audience, it would also establish a foundation of understanding in London. I already knew that some of these artists would be present in the Whitechapel programme. In 1980, before 'A New Spirit in Painting' was really fully conceived, I was already working on a Philip Guston show, for instance. We recognised that the exhibition was taking place in London, but the ambition was to address the international audience.

I think that Christos, Norman and I all felt that it would be possible to present a rather classical exhibition devoted to painting in the beautiful top-lit galleries of the Royal

Academy, in a way that would be very striking and quite unlike an exhibition that you might do in a Kunsthalle in Germany, or even at the documenta or at the Venice Biennale. The classic character of those spaces immediately created a dialogue with the whole history of painting. For us, this was a very important feature of the show. When we were trying to persuade the Academy that they should endorse the exhibition that we had in mind, part of the argument was to say to the Academy that it had a responsibility to renew an appetite for painting and sculpture in every generation.

TdL *You have just mentioned sculpture. At the Whitechapel, you also presented the exhibition 'British Sculpture in the Twentieth Century' in 1981 and you organised the exhibition 'In-Tandem' in 1987, which was focused on artists who are both painters and sculptors. Many of the artists included in 'A New Spirit in Painting' are as much sculptors as they are painters: Picasso, de Kooning, Baselitz, Kiefer, Schnabel, Kirkeby or Twombly. To what extent was sculpture theoretically necessary when* you *were conceptualising 'A New Spirit in Painting'? Did the idea of doing an exhibition on artists who are painters and sculptors arise in 1981?*

NS The idea of doing 'In-Tandem' was not in my mind in 1981. Personally, I have always been attracted to sculpture, though I recognise that sculpture is much less appreciated by a general audience than painting. My interest was probably encouraged by working on more than one occasion with David Sylvester, who had also a very strong feeling for sculpture. I worked with him on an exhibition on Miró's sculptures at the Hayward Gallery in 1972 and learned so much about how you place sculpture in space.

I became more and more interested in the phenomenon of the painter/sculptor as I realised that painters have made such an important contribution to the history of sculpture in the twentieth century. Many of the most important transformations in our understanding of sculpture had been achieved by painters. So in about 1982 or 1983, I decided I should try to make an exhibition at the Whitechapel when we re-opened after renovation. I worked with Lynne Cooke on the show.

TdL *Which studios did you visit while you were organising 'A New Spirit in Painting'? Can you recount the most decisive studio visits?*

NS I remember two studio visits in particular. One to a studio I had never been to before and one to a studio which I had visited previously.

The studio I had been to before was the studio of Robert Ryman, which was a very spectacular space in Greenwich Street in New York. It was a space that had previously been used by scenic artists working on canvases for theatre. It was on two levels and it was possible to lift and bring down large theatrical canvases attached to movable frames. Ryman worked in this space on really quite small paintings. The reason I remember it is because in the conversation with Norman and Christos, I remember quite a debate about whether or not to include in this exhibition artists like Ryman, Marden and so on. These artists had been making painting from the mid-1960s into the 1970s. The language they were using was not really regarded as the language of painting until the mid-1970s when slowly a small number of exhibitions brought some of these minimalist painters together. For instance, there was an important show at the Stedelijk Museum Amsterdam in 1975 called 'Fundamental Painting'. In the conceiving of the exhibition at the Royal Academy, which was seen as an exhibition which would survey the whole language of painting, there seemed to be great energy and a new language in this form of painting. Christos admired, for instance, the very early monochrome paintings of Kounellis, which were not included in the exhibition because they were too early. But he was not quite sure whether or not we should stretch the exhibition in this way. We went to Ryman's studio together. I think he was taken by the rigour and energy of Ryman's activity. I think that he found in this intensity a very different kind of expression but also an intensity similar to the one of the next artist I am going to talk about.

I also remember very strongly the visit to Derneburg. Norman had been previously to Derneburg and I had not been. Norman insisted on having a little piece of theatre as we arrived. We had a hire car, we all met in Hannover and we drove to Derneburg. As we entered the village, Norman insisted on putting a tape into the cassette recorder and on came Wagner, as a prelude to arriving at the castle! For me, what was really striking about Baselitz was the experience of being in the grand hall that he was using as a studio, and seeing him working with incredible energy on these eight or ten canvases, all upside down. I had seen paintings in exhibitions, of course, I had seen small gallery shows but I had never seen a big exhibition. I was really astonished by what I saw. In another room he was working on a sculpture of a large wooden figure – the sculpture that was shown to some controversy in the German Pavilion at the Venice Biennale in 1980.

TdL *The 1980 Venice Biennale was quite decisive with regard to 'A New Spirit in Painting'. You were speaking about the Royal Academy as a place that allows for a dialogue between the past and the now. Venice too is a place where different periods of history mingle. The artists invited to the Venice Biennale dialogue with the great Venetian masters: Tiziano, Veronese, Tintoretto. Maybe one could say that the painters included in 'A New Spirit in Painting' are more Venetian than they are Florentine. Among the paintings you included in the exhibition, Richter's series stems from Tiziano's* Annunciation, *which is in the collection of the Scuola Grande di San Rocco. How crucial was the 1980 Venice Biennale?*

NS When we decided to include some artists from an earlier generation, the discussion was influenced by the experience of visiting Venice together. We did not go to the opening in Venice but later because we wanted to look very carefully at the contributions of particular artists. This was the moment when Harald Szeemann was showing the emerging *Transavanguardia*. The experience of Venice reinforced the insight that we had to deal with several generations. The younger generation were very consciously looking at the previous generations and especially at the work of their "grandfathers".

This was also the moment when people began to recognise that the late works of Picasso had a strength and a quality which had been overlooked. Of course, there had been the big exhibitions in Avignon but everyone dismissed these late works, as the works of an old man. Somehow the sensibility changed from 1978. We did not know at that time that Christian Geelhaar was proposing to make the exhibition of late Picasso in Basel in 1981, probably the first exhibition which looked really seriously at the late works. Frankly, I don't think we represented Picasso in the exhibition as strongly as we could have done. Four paintings were in the central hall. *Child with a Spade* is a particularly wonderful painting [looks at the painting in the exhibition catalogue]. But even to include these paintings was regarded as a surprising thing to do at that moment.

TdL *Yet it was paradoxically thought that Picasso was used as an argument from authority in the exhibition. The exhibition and the artists in it were heavily criticised in the 1980s, especially in America through the articles published in the journal* October. *The exhibition was castigated as regressive and reactionary. What idea of modernity did you want to convey? What vision of painting did you want to express? What was your theoretical approach as you were curating the exhibition?*

NS I think the curatorial formulation of the exhibition was not established on the basis of having a single theoretical positon, which we then sought to justify by the choices. I think it was driven in part by a feeling that painting, the language of painting, could not be limited solely to abstraction and to a rather pure modernist vision of abstraction. There was also a belief that painting could more directly address questions of history and of society. For me, it was very necessary to make a statement that Baselitz and Kiefer, but also Guston in America, were changing the accepted notions of what the limits of painting could be. Guston himself had been repudiated by most critics in America with a modernist sensibility. Their position seemed to have extinguished the possibility of there being an ostensible subject in painting.

TdL *Some of the paintings included in 'A New Spirit in Painting' engage with history in two ways. One may be quite superficial and addresses the problems formulated after the war – which is the aspect embraced by much of the critics of the 1970s and the 1980s, one which is a deeper bond with history – the reflection of the history of painting or the remembrance of things past.*

NS You mentioned the Richters. As I said earlier, one of the appealing things about doing the exhibition at the Royal Academy was that it immediately obliged you to consider the whole relationship between contemporary painting and painting of the past. At certain moments, Richter has very self-consciously connected himself to the history of painting. At the Whitechapel, we had presented a group of recent abstract paintings together with a very small group of much earlier paintings from the 1960s based on photographs, partly because I wanted to make the point that he worked in different modes. In 'A New Spirit' it seemed an interesting idea to take Richter as one of those artists self-consciously placing themselves in the history of painting.

TdL *It seems that in 1981 you interpreted the works included in the exhibition in quite different terms than those of Norman and Christos.*

NS I am not a historian but I am interested in how patterns of thought reoccur in different generations, emerge and have influence from one generation to the next. I am interested in the way in which artists commit on society. For me the best do it in a very oblique way, which is often fractured and broken, not based on direct description.

TdL *Was there any artist you did not manage to include in 'A New Spirit in Painting'?*

NS We had a very big debate about Susan Rothenberg. Undoubtedly, there was a moment when she could easily have been included in the show. There was also a big debate about Jasper Johns. The decisive opponent to Jasper Johns was

Christos. I think it had to do with the fact that he felt that the paintings Johns was making at that time, the crosshatch paintings, were nothing like as strong as the paintings he had been making the 1960s and the early 1970s. Christos felt strongly that the inclusion of Johns would show an artist who had come down from a height and was not ascending to a height.

With hindsight, I think we could easily have made a case for including Beuys, especially with the inclusion of Merz and Kounellis. I rather regret that Beuys was not included. Drawings or works on paper but also works that have a connection with painting could have been included.

TdL *You got to organise exhibitions on the same artists at different times in your career. One could think of Kirkeby, Richter or Twombly. How has your understanding of their work shifted over the past years? Has your vision changed?*

NS At the time of 'A New Spirit in Painting', I had known the work of many of these artists for five or six years. In 1972, I began to move beyond the artists of my generation with whom I was immediately working to think about different kinds of language and different kinds of artists – especially when I started to discover Polke, Penck and others working in Germany from 1973 onwards.

I have made a second exhibition with some of those artists in a different context and primarily because I became more and more intrigued by and interested in the depth and the resonance of their work. For an artist like Kirkeby, initially, I really did not understand what he was doing and why. Even an artist like Cy Twombly: I really began to understand Twombly more fully when I went to visit him in Lexington. I understood his connection with Southern culture, the literary traditions of Lexington and the Washington and Lee University, the white-painted buildings, the wooden houses, the light, the nature and the landscape.

When you make a really big exhibition with an artist and you work with him or her for two or three years, by the end of the exhibition, you really do understand this artist, you fully

comprehend them in some way. Then, a few years later you are going to realise that you did not understand everything at all, which is why we keep on looking at Shakespeare at different ages in our lives.
For an artist like Gerhard Richter, I made three exhibitions: one in Whitechapel in 1979, one at the Tate in 1990 and one at the Tate again in 2011. By the time I had finished making the exhibition in 2011, you might think my appetite for him would be somehow fulfilled or satisfied. But by the end of the exhibition, I still felt that this is a really mysterious and admirable mind. I could make another exhibition that would be totally different.

TdL *How you would view the exhibition from today's vantage point – is it more relevant than ever? Or, did its message get through and is seen everywhere today?*

NS We know that certain parts of the message came through. One was to break down the hierarchies that had existed, in the museums and in the market in regard to German art in particular. Clearly, as a result of the exhibition, there was also a renewed interest and faith in painting as a means of expression.

The exhibition also provided an opportunity to reassess the work of some senior artists. At the end of the 1970s, there was a certain respect for an artist like Bacon but that respect was largely founded on the paintings that he had made in the 1950s rather than the recent paintings. So, one of the legacies of the exhibition was the interest in the concept of 'late work'. Although the idea of a focus on late works was not provoked solely by 'A New Spirit in Painting', the exhibition helped to break down some of the accepted criteria about how you judge artists. For most of the twentieth-century artists were held in high regard because of they had made a formal breakthrough or initiated a new language. Late work was not something that was highly valued in the twentieth century. You might tolerate the late Picasso, you might tolerate the late Matisse. But if you had to choose between a Matisse late cut-out and a painting from 1914 or 1917, you would choose the early work. 'A New Spirit' helped to change the balance of how we think about the trajectory of artists and it changed the terms of the debate about what constitutes significance in painting.

'A New Spirit in Painting'
took place at the Royal Academy of Arts, London

Dates of the exhibition:
15 January – 18 March 1981

Committee of Honor	Professor Alan Bowness Dominique Bozo Dr. Luigi Carluccio Thomas M. Messer Prof. Dr. Wieland Schmied Prof. Dr. Stephan Waetzoldt
Organizers of the Exhibition	Christos M. Joachimides Norman Rosenthal Nicholas Serota
Artists in the Exhibition	Frank Auerbach Francis Bacon Balthus Georg Baselitz Pier Paolo Calzolari Alan Charlton Sandro Chia Rainer Fetting Lucian Freud Gotthard Graubner Philip Guston Dieter Hacker Jean Hélion David Hockney Howard Hodgkin K.H. Hödicke

Anselm Kiefer
Per Kirkeby
R.B. Kitaj
Bernd Koberling
Willem de Kooning
Jannis Kounellis
Markus Lüpertz
Brice Marden
Matta
Bruce McLean
Mario Merz
Malcolm Morley
Mimmo Paladino
A.R. Penck
Pablo Picasso
Sigmar Polke
Gerhard Richter
Robert Ryman
Julian Schnabel
Frank Stella
Cy Twombly
Andy Warhol

Lenders to the Exhibition

Kunstmuseum Basel, Basel
Berlinische Galerie, Berlin
Staatliche Museen Preußischer Kulturbesitz, Nationalgalerie, Berlin
Museum Ludwig, Cologne
Scottish National Gallery of Modern Art, Edinburgh
Stedelijk van Abbemuseum, Eindhoven
Staatliche Kunstsammlungen Kassel, Neue Galerie
Tate Gallery, London
Musée Picasso, Paris
Boymans-Van Beuningen Museum, Rotterdam

Thomas Amman, Zürich
Francis Bacon, London
Karen and Jean Bernier, Athens
Bruno Bischofberger, Kussnacht/Zürich
Galerie Bruno Bischofberger, Kussnacht/Zürich
Marlies Black, New York
Mary Boone, New York
Mary Boone Gallery, New York
Udo and Annette Brandhorst, Cologne
A. R. Burki, Solothurn
Alan Charlton, London
Crex Collection, Zürich
Anthony d'Offay Gallery, London
B. J. Eastwood
Theodore J. Edlich, Jr, New York
Rainer Fetting, Berlin
Konrad Fischer, Düsseldorf
Xavier Fourcade, Inc, New York
The Estate of Philip Guston, New York
Mr. And Mrs. Richard C. Hedreen, Seattle
Jacqueline Hélion, Bigeonnette
David Hockney, London/Los Angeles
K. H. Hödicke, Berlin
Mr. and Mrs. Edward R. Hudson, Jr, Fort Worth/Texas
Alexander Iolas, Athens
Barbara Jakobson, New York
Anselm Kiefer, Hornbach, Odenwald
James Kirman, London
Bernd Koberling
Jannis Kounellis, Rome
Lafrenz Collection, Hamburg
Galerie Yvon Lambert, Paris
Marlborough Fine Art, London

Francesco Masnata, Genoa
Matta, Tarquinia
Bruce McLean, London
Samuel A. McLean, London
Mario Merz, Turin
Robert Miller, New York
Galerie Neuendorf, Hamburg
Galleria Franz Paludetto, Turin
Bernard Ruiz Picasso, Paris
Hélène Rochas, Paris
Lawrence Rubin, New York
Julian Schnabel, New York
Ileana Sonnabend, New York
Gian Enzo Sperone, Turin
H. H. Stober, Berlin
Thyssen-Bornemisza Collection, Lugano
Michel Tournier, Choisel
Richard L. Weisman, New York
Galerie Michael Werner, New York
David Whitney, New York
Mayen and Chlodwig Würdig, Wilzhofen

Bibliography

A

Adriani, G.
– *The Early Years of the Old Masters: Baselitz - Richter - Polke - Kiefer* (exh. cat. Staatsgalerie Stuttgart, Deichtorhallen Hamburg), Stuttgart and Hamburg 2019.

Ammann, J.-C.
Brock, B. Szeemann, H.
– 'Second Concept for *documenta 5*', in *Harald Szeemann. Individual Methodology* (Zürich: JRP|Ringier Kunstverlag AG, 2007).

Apollinaire, G.
– *Calligrammes* (Paris: Mercure de France, 1918).

Arasse, D.
– 'Les Miroirs de Cindy Sherman', *artpress*, Vol. 245 (1999), pp. 24-30.
– *Anselm Kiefer*, trans. by Whittall, M. (London: Thames & Hudson, 2001).
– 'Le tableau préféré', Histoire de peintures (2003), France Culture. Available at https://www.franceculture.fr/histoire/histoires-de-peintures-le-tableau-prefere (Accessed 9 December 2017).

B

Barr, A. Jr
– 'Introduction' in *The New American Painting* (exh. cat. The Museum of Modern Art), New York 1959, pp. 15-19.

Barthes, R.
– *Leçon* (Paris: Éditions du Seuil, 1978).
–'Lecture in Inauguration of the Chair of Literary Semiology, Collège de France, January 7, 1977', trans. by Howard R. *October*, Vol. 8 (1979), pp. 3-16.

– 'Cy Twombly ou *Non multa sed multum*' in *L'Obvie et l'obtus. Essais critiques III* (Paris: Éditions du Seuil, coll. « Tel Quel », 1982), pp. 145-162.
–'Sagesse de l'art' in *L'Obvie et l'obtus. Essais critiques III* (Paris: Éditions du Seuil, coll. « Tel Quel », 1982), pp. 163-178.
– Œuvres complètes, ed. Marty, É. (Vol. 3) (Paris: Seuil, 2002).

Baudelaire, C.
– *Les Fleurs du mal in Œuvres complètes* (Paris: Gallimard, coll. « Bibliothèque de la Pléiade », 1954), pp. 77-203.

Benjamin, W.
– *Gesammelte Schriften. Band II* (Frankfurt am Main: Suhrkamp Verlag, 1977).
– *The Arcades Project*, trans. by Eiland, H. and McLaughlin, K. (Cambridge, MA: Harvard University Press, 1999).
– 'Goethe's *Elective Affinities' in Selected Writings: Volume* 1, 1913–1926, ed. Bullock, M. and Jennings M. W. (London: Belknap Press of Harvard University Press, 2004), pp. 297-360.

Bernabò, M.
– *Il Fisiologo di Smirne* (Florence: Sismel Edizioni del Galluzzo, 1998).

Bois, Y.-A.
– 'Ryman's Tact', *October*, Vol. 19 (1981), pp. 93-104.
– 'Surprise and Equanimity' in *Robert Ryman: Critical Texts Since 1967* (London: Ridinghouse, 2009), pp. 230-243.

Bourel, M.
– 'Art Conceptuel' in *Art conceptuel* I (exh. cat. CAPC Musée d'Art Contemporain de Bordeaux), Bordeaux 1988, pp. 9-12.

Buchloh, B. H. D.
– 'Figures of Authority, Ciphers of Regression: Notes on the Return of Representation in European Painting', *October*, Vol. 16 (1981), pp. 39-68.
– 'The Posters in Lawrence Weiner' in *Neo-Avantgarde and Culture Industry* (Cambridge, MA: The MIT Press, 2000), pp. 555-576.
– '1972a' in ed. Foster, H. Krauss, R. Bois Y.-A. Buchloh B. H. D. Joselit D. Art Since 1900: *Modernism, Antimodernism, Postmodernism* (London: Thames & Hudson, 2004), pp. 549-553.

Burke, E.
– *Reflections on the French Revolution* (London: J.M. Dent & Sons Ltd., 1910).

C

Calvocoressi, R.
– Anselm Kiefer *Uraeus* (exh. cat. Gagosian), New York 2019.

Chateaubriand, R.
– *Memoirs of Chateaubriand* (London: Henry Colburn Publisher, 1849).

Cohn, D.
– 'Anselm Kiefer, un parcours en perspective', *Communications*, Vol. 85 (2009), pp. 117-125.
– 'La Matière de la mémoire: Daniel Arasse et Anselm Kiefer' in *Daniel Arasse. Historien de l'art* (Paris: INHA - Les Éditions des Cendres, 2010), pp. 257-270.

Compagnon, A.
– *Les Antimodernes* (Paris: Gallimard, coll. « Bibliothèque des Idées », 2005).

Crimp, D.
– 'The End of painting', *October*, Vol. 16 (1981), pp. 69-86

Crow, T.
– *Modern Art in Common Culture* (New Haven, CT & London: Yale University Press, 1996).

D

Dagen, P.
– 'Un moderne chez les contemporains' in *Daniel Arasse. Historien de l'art* (Paris: INHA - Les Éditions des Cendres, 2010), pp. 271-280.

Damisch, H.
– 'The Duchamp Defense', trans by. Krauss, R. *October*, Vol. 10 (1979), pp. 5-28.
– 'Stratégies, 1950-1960' in *Fenêtre jaune cadmium. Ou les dessous de la peinture* (Paris: Éditions du Seuil, coll. « Fiction & Cie », 1984), pp. 142-179.
– *The Judgment of Paris*, trans. by John Goodman (Chicago, IL & London: The University of Chicago Press, 1996).

– 'Dubuffet or the Reading of the World', trans. by Minturn, K. and Wadhera, P. *Art in Translation*, Vol. 6 No. 3 (2014), pp. 299-316.
– 'Quant au titre. Cy Twombly', in *La Ruse du tableau: La peinture ou ce qu'il en reste* (Paris: Seuil, coll. « La Librairie du XXIe siècle », 2016), pp. 37-58.
– 'Attention: fragile: Ad Reinhardt' in *La Ruse du tableau: La peinture ou ce qu'il en reste* (Paris: Seuil, coll. « La Librairie du XXIe siècle », 2016), pp. 131-136.
– 'La déplacée' in *La Ruse du tableau: La peinture ou ce qu'il en reste* (Paris: Seuil, coll. « La Librairie du XXIe siècle », 2016), pp. 217-231.

Darragon, É.
– 'Someone Else: Between History and Utopia' in *The Michael Werner Collection* (exh. cat. Musée d'Art Moderne de la Ville de Paris), Paris 2012, pp. 27-33.

de Duve, T.
– *Nominalisme pictural. Marcel Duchamp, la peinture et la modernité* (Paris: Les Éditions de Minuit, coll. « Critique », 2014).

Deleuze, G.
– *Francis Bacon: Logique de la sensation* (Paris: Seuil, coll. « L'Ordre philosophique », 2002).
– *Francis Bacon: The Logic of Sensation*, trans. by David W. Smith (London & New York, NY: Continuum, 2003).

Derrida, J.
– *La Vérité en peinture* (Paris: Flammarion, 1978).
– 'Heidegger's Hand (Geschlecht II)', trans. by Leavey, Jr, J. P. and Rottenberg, E. in *Psyche: Inventions of the Other, Volume II*, ed. Kamuf, P. and Rottenberg, E. (Stanford, CA: Stanford University Press, 2008), pp. 27-62.

Didi-Huberman, G.
– 'The art of not describing: Vermeer: the detail and the patch', trans. by Cheal Pugh, A. *History of the Human Sciences*, Vol. 2 No. 2 (1989), pp. 135-169.
– *Ce que nous voyons, ce qui nous regarde* (Paris: Les Éditions de Minuit, coll. « Critique », 1992)
– 'Notre Dibbouk. Aby Warburg dans l'autre temps de l'histoire', *La Part de l'oeil*, No. 15-16 (1999-2000).
– 'The Imaginary breeze: Remarks on the air of the Quattrocento', trans. by Zeimbekis, J. and Rehberg, V. *Journal of visual culture*, Vol. No. 3 (2003), pp. 275-289.

Dolce, L.
– *Dialogo della pittura. Intitolato l'Aretino* (Venice: Gabriel Giolito de' Ferrari, 1557).

Dubreuil-Blondin, N.
– 'Feminism and Modernism: Paradoxes' in *Modernism and Modernity* (Halifax, Nova Scotia: The Press of the Nova Scotia College of Art and Design, 1983), pp. 195-211.

F

Faroult, G.
– '"The Dreams of a Contemporary Man": Contemporary Perspective' in *Hubert Robert, 1733-1808* (exh. cat. Musée du Louvre, National Gallery of Art), Washington, DC 2016, pp. 23-31

Flynt, H.
– 'Concept Art' in *An Anthology of Chance and Operations*, ed. Young, L.M. (New York, NY: Young & Jackson Mac Low, 1963).

Focillon, H.
– *La Vie des formes* (Paris: Presses Universitaires de France, 1947)

Foster, H.
– *Recodings: Art, Spectacle, Cultural Politics* (Seattle, WA: Bay Press, 1985).
– '1984' in ed. Foster, H. Krauss, R. Bois Y.-A. Buchloh B. H. D. Joselit D. *Art Since 1900: Modernism, Antimodernism, Postmodernism* (3rd edition) (London: Thames & Hudson, 2016), pp. 698-701.

Fried, M.
– "Some New Category": Remarks on Several Black Pollocks' in *Jackson Pollock: Blind Spots* (exh. cat. Tate Gallery Liverpool), Liverpool 2015, pp. 57-71.

Froment, J.-L.
– *Légendes* (exh. cat. CAPC Musée d'Art contemporain de Bordeaux), Bordeaux 1984.

G

Ginzburg, C.
– 'Morelli, Freud and Sherlock Holmes: Clues and Scientific Method', *History Workshop*, No. 9 (1980), pp. 5-36.

Gombrich, E.
– *Aby Warburg: An Intellectual Biography* (Oxford: Phaidon, 1986).

Greenberg, C.
– 'Abstract and Representational', in *The Collected Essays and Criticism. Affirmations and Refusals, 1950-1966* (Vol. 3) (Chicago, IL: The University of Chicago Press, 1993), pp. 186-193.
– 'Modernist Painting' in *The Collected Essays and Criticism. Modernism with a Vengeance*, 1957-1969 (Vol. 4) (Chicago, IL: The University of Chicago Press, 1993), pp. 84-93.

Gropius, W.
– *The Scope of Total Architecture* (New York, NY: Collier Books, 1962).

Guston, P.
– 'Piero della Francesca: The Impossibility of Painting' in Guston, P. *Collected Writings, Lectures, and Conversations* (Berkeley, CA: University of California Press, 2011), p. 41.

H

Habermas, J.
– 'Modernity – An Incomplete Project' in *The Anti-Aesthetic: Essays on Postmodern Culture*, ed. Foster, H. (Port Townsend, WA: Bay Press, 1983), pp. 3-15.

Harrison, C.
– "Seeing' and 'Describing': the Artist's Studio' in *Essays on Art & Language* (Oxford: Basil Blackwell Ltd, 1991), pp. 150-174.

K

Kaschnitz-Weinberg, G.
– 'Review of Alois Riegl, *Die Spätrömische Kunstindustrie*, 1927', trans. by Martin Schwarz, *Art History*, Vol. 39 No. 1 (2016), pp. 84-97.

Kneubühler, T.
– 'Markus Lüpertz: Pintura de elusión' in *Markus Lüpertz: Retrospectiva 1963-1990* (exh. cat. Museo Reina Sofia), Madrid 1993, pp. 24-29.

Kozloff, M.
– 'The Authoritarian Personality in Modern Art', *Artforum*, Vol. 12 No. 9 (1974).

Krauss, R.
– '1972' in ed. Foster, H. Krauss, R. Bois Y.-A. Buchloh B. H. D. Joselit D. *Art Since 1900: Modernism, Antimodernism, Postmodernism* (3rd edition) (London: Thames & Hudson, 2016), pp. 672-675.

Krens, T.
– 'German Painting: Paradox and Paradigm in Late Twentieth-Century Art', in *Refigured Painting: The German Image 1960-88* (exh. cat. The Solomon R. Guggenheim Museum), New York 1989, pp. 12-21.

Kuspit, D.B.
– 'Acts of Aggression: German Painting Today, Part 1', *Art in America*, (September 1982), pp. 140-151.
– 'Flak from the "Radicals": The American Case Against Current German Painting', in *Expressions: New Art from Germany* (exh. cat. The Saint Louis Museum). Saint Louis, MO, 1983, pp. 42-55.

L

Lebensztejn, J.-C.
– 'Framing Classical Space', *Art Journal*, Vol. 47 No. 1 (1988), pp. 37-41.

Lefebvre, H.
– 'Modernity and Modernism' in *Modernism and Modernity* (Halifax, Nova Scotia: The Press of the Nova Scotia College of Art and Design, 1983), pp. 1-3.

Leiris, M.
– *Francis Bacon*, trans. by Weightman, J. (Barcelona: Ediciones Polígrafa, 2008).

Lévi-Strauss, C.
– 'Le métier perdu', Le Débat, Vol. 10 (1981), pp. 5-9.
– *Le Regard éloigné* (Paris: Plon, 1983).
– *La Voie des masques* in *Œuvres* (Paris: Gallimard, coll. « Bibliothèque de la Pléiade », 2008), pp. 873-1052.

Lippard, L.
– *From the Center: Feminist Essays on Women's Art* (New York, NY: Dutton, 1976).

Lippard, L. Chandler, J.
– 'The Dematerialisation of Art', *Art International*, Vol. 12 No. 2 (1968), pp. 31-36.

Lukinovitch, A.
– 'Homenaje a Markus Lüpertz. La nueva musa' in *Markus Lüpertz: Retrospectiva 1963-1990* (exh. cat. Museo Reina Sofia), Madrid 1993, pp. 30-31.

Lyotard, J.-F.
– *Discourse, Figure*, trans. by Hudek, A. and Lydon, M. (Minneapolis, MN: University of Minnesota Press, 2011).

M

Malraux, A.
– *Le Miroir des limbes* (Paris: Gallimard, 1976).

Marin, L.
– 'La description du tableau et le sublime en peinture', *Communications*, No. 34 (1981), pp. 61-84.
– *Le Portrait du roi* (Paris: Les Éditions de Minuit, coll. « Le Sens commun », 1981).
– 'Un peintre sous influences : Notes sur « de Kooning et la tradition flamande et hollandaise de peinture »' in *Willem de Kooning* (exh. cat. Centre Georges Pompidou - Musée national d'art moderne), Paris 1984, pp. 31-39.
– 'Le Cadre de la représentation et quelques-unes de ses figures', *Les Cahiers du Musée National d'Art Moderne*, No. 24 (1988), pp. 62-81.
– 'Frontiers of Utopia: Past and Present', *Critical Inquiry*, Vol. 19, No. 3 (1993), pp. 397-420.

McEvilley, T.
– 'I Think Therefore I Art', *Artforum*, Vol. 23 No. 10 (1985), pp. 74-85.

Meuli, A.
– 'Georg Baselitz: «Adler» Motiv und künstlerischer Akt', *Artefactum*, Vol. 4 No. 19 (1987), pp. 24-27.

N

Nancy, J.-L.
– 'Le vestige de l'art' in *Les Muses* (Paris: Editions Galilée, 2001), pp. 133-160.

Nietzsche, F.
– 'On the Uses and Disadvantages of History for Life' in *Untimely Meditations*, trans. by Hollingdale R.J. (Cambridge: Cambridge University Press, 1997), pp. 59-123.

O

Ottinger, D.
– 'Picasso: An Embarrassing Heritage' in *Picasso.Mania* (exh. cat. Réunion des Musées Nationaux - Grand Palais), Paris 2016, p. 228-236.

P

Panofsky, E.
– *Idea: ein Beitrag zur Begriffsgeschichte der älteren Kunsttheorie* (Leipzig: Teubner, 1924).
– *Albrecht Dürer: Volume One* (Princeton, NJ: Princeton University Press, 1945).
– 'The Concept of Artistic Volition', trans. by Kenneth Northcott and Joel Snyder, *Critical Inquiry*, Vol. 8. No. 1 (1981), pp. 17-33.

Pasolini, P. P.
– *Poesia in forma di rosa* (1961-1964) (Milan: Garzanti, 1964)

Poussin, N.
– *Collection de lettres de Nicolas Poussin*, ed. de Quincy, Q. (Paris: Firmin Didot, 1824).

Proust, M
– *On Reading Ruskin*, ed. Wolfe, P. J. Burford, W. (New Haven, CT & London: Yale University Press, 1989).
– *À la recherche du temps perdu*, Vol. III, *Le Côté de Guermantes* (Paris: Gallimard, coll. « Blanche », 1992).
– *À la recherche du temps perdu*, Vol. VII, *Le Temps retrouvé* (Paris: Gallimard, coll. « Blanche », 1992).

R

Rampley, M.
– *The Remembrance of Things Past: On Aby M. Warburg and Walter Benjamin* (Wiesbaden: Harrasowitz Verlag, 2000).

Reinhardt, A.
– 'Art-as-Art' in *Art-as-Art: The Selected Writing of Ad Reinhardt* (Berkeley, CA: University of California Press, 1991), pp. 53-63.

Rilke, R.M.
– *Duino Elegies*, trans. by Leishman, J.B. and Spender, S. (London: Hogarth Press, 1942).

Rishel, J.
– 'The Culture of Painting: Guston and History' in *Philip Guston Retrospective* (exh. cat. Royal Academy of Arts), London 2003, pp. 75-82.

Rosenthal, N.
– 'A Will to Art in Twentieth Century Germany' in *German Art in the Twentieth Century: Painting and Sculpture* (exh. cat. Royal Academy of Arts), London 1985, pp. 13-20.

Rosenthal, M.
– *Anselm Kiefer* (exh. cat. The Art Institute of Chicago & the Philadelphia Museum of Art), Chicago and Philadelphia 1987.

Roy, C.
– *Balthus*, trans. by Ann Sautier-Greening (Boston and London: Little, Brown and Company, 1996).

S

Schmidt, K.
– 'Immortal and Eternally Young' in *Twombly and Poussin: Arcadian Painters* (exh. cat. Dulwich Picture Gallery), London 2011, pp. 65-85.

Serota, N.
– 'Anselm Kiefer: Les Plaintes d'un Icare (From the Poem by Baudelaire 1862)' in *Anselm Kiefer* (exh. cat. Whitechapel Gallery, Museum Folkwang), London and Essen 1981, pp. 19-23.

Shiff, R.
– 'Georg Baselitz Grounded', *Art Institute of Chicago Museum Studies*, Vol. 28 No. 1 (2002), pp. 52-65, 109-110.

Simondon, G.
– *On the Mode of Existence of Technical Objects*, trans. by Malaspina, C. and Rogove, J. (Minneapolis, MN: University of Minnesota Press, 2016).

Slifkin, R.
– *Out of Time: Philip Guston and the Refiguration of Postwar American Art* (Berkeley, CA: University of California Press, 2013).

Storr, R.
– 'Simple Gifts' in *Robert Ryman* (exh. cat. Tate Gallery, Museum of Modern Art), London & New York 1993, pp. 9-45.
– *Gerhard Richter: Forty Years of Painting* (exh. cat Museum of Modern Art), New York 2002.

Strzygowski, J.
– *Der Bilderkreis des griechischen Physiologus* (Leipzig: Druck und Verlag von B.G. Teubner, 1899).

Suthor, N.
– *Bravura: Virtuosität und Mutwilligkeit in der Malerei der frühen Neuzeit* (München: Wilhelm Fink, 2010).

Sweeney, J. J.
– 'Eleven Painters in America. Interview with Marcel Duchamp', *The Museum of Modern Art Bulletin*, Vol. 13 No. 4-5 (1946), pp. 19-21.

Sylvester, D
– *The Brutality of Fact: Interviews with Francis Bacon* (3rd enlarged edition) (Oxford: Thames & Hudson, 1987).
– 'Flesh Was the Reason' in *Willem de Kooning: Paintings*, ed. Marla Prather (exh. cat. National Gallery of Art), Washington, DC 1994.

T

– *Twombly and Poussin: Arcadian Painters* (exh. cat. Dulwich Picture Gallery), London 2011.

W

Waldman, D.
– 'Georg Baselitz: Art on the Edge' in *Georg Baselitz* (exh. cat. The Solomon R. Guggenheim Museum) New York 1995, pp. 1-210.

Weiner, L.
– *Displacement* (exh. cat. Dia Art Foundation), New York 1991.

List of Illustrations

8 **Francis Bacon**
Landscape, 1978
Oil and pastel on canvas
198 x 147,5 cm
Private Collection

9 **Paul Cézanne**
Château noir, 1900-1904
Oil on canvas
74 x 96,5 cm
National Gallery of Art, Washington D.C.

10 **Philip Guston**
Door, 1978
Oil on canvas
172,5 x 277 cm
Stedelijk Museum, Amsterdam

11 **Piero della Francesca**
Flagellazione, 1459-1460
Tempera on panel
58,4 cm x 81,5 cm
Galleria Nazionale delle Marche, Urbino

12 **Georg Baselitz**
Fingermalerei-Adler, 1972
Oil on canvas
249,5 x 180,3 cm
Bayerische Staatsgemäldesammlungen,
Sammlung Moderne Kunst in der Pinakothek
der Moderne, München

13 **Jean Siméon Chardin**
Nature morte au faisan et gibecière, 1760
Oil on canvas
72,8 x 60,4 cm
Staatliche Museen zu Berlin,
Gemäldegalerie, Berlin

14 **Chaïm Soutine**
Dead Fowl, 1926
Oil on canvas
97,5 x 63,3 cm
The Art Institute of Chicago, Chicago

15 Peter Paul Rubens
The Abduction of Ganymede, 1611-1612
Oil on canvas
207 x 207 cm
The Liechtenstein Museum, Vienna

16 *Smyrna Physiologus*, Twelfth Century AD

17 Chaïm Soutine
Groupe d'arbres, 1922
Oil on canvas
73,3 x 60,6 cm
The Barnes Foundation, Philadelphia

18 Willem de Kooning
Untitled II, 1977
Oil on canvas
195,5 x 223,5 cm
Private Collection

19 Georg Baselitz
Fingermalerei-Adler (detail), 1972
Oil on Canvas, 249,5 x 180,3 cm
Bayerische Staatsgemäldesammlungen,
Sammlung Moderne Kunst in der Pinakothek
der Moderne, München

20 Gerhard Richter
Verkündigung nach Tizian (344-3), 1973
Oil on canvas
150 cm x 250 cm
Kunstmuseum Basel, Basel

21 Tiziano
Annunciazione, 1535
Oil on canvas
166 x 266 cm
Scuola Grande di San Rocco, Venezia

22 Pablo Picasso
Child with a Spade [*Enfant à la pelle*]
Mougins, 15 July and 14 November, 1971
Oil on canvas
195 x 130 cm
Fundación Almine y Bernard Ruiz-Picasso
para el Arte, Madrid

23 **Albrecht Dürer**
Melencolia I, 1514
Engraving
27 x 21,6 cm
Musée Condé, Chantilly

24 **Andy Warhol**
Ileana Sonnabend, 1973
Acrylic and silkscreen ink on canvas
Diptych, each panel: 101,6 x 203,2 cm
The Sonnabend Collection

25 **Sandro Botticelli**
Giuliano de' Medici, 1478
Oil on Canvas
57,1 x 38,4 cm
Staatliche Museen zu Berlin,
Gemäldegalerie, Berlin

26 **Rainer Fetting**
Große Dusche (Panorama), 1981
Dispersion paint on canvas
289 cm × 491 cm
Staatliche Museen zu Berlin,
Hamburger Bahnhof - Museum für Gegenwart,
Sammlung Dr. Erich Marx, Berlin

CREDITS

Every effort has been made to supply complete and correct credits; if there are errors or omissions, please contact the publisher so that corrections can be made in any subsequent editions.

Figure 1: Markus Lüpertz © VG Bild-Kunst, Bonn 2019 – Figure 4: Lawrence Weiner © VG Bild-Kunst, Bonn 2019 – Figure 5: © Pollock-Krasner Foundation / VG Bild-Kunst, Bonn 2019 – Figure 6: © Balthus – Figure 7: Robert Ryman © VG Bild-Kunst, Bonn 2019. Photo: courtesy Daros Collection, Switzerland – Figure 8: © The Estate of Francis Bacon. All rights reserved / VG Bild-Kunst, Bonn 2019. Photo: Prudence Cuming Associates Ltd – Figure 10: © The Estate of Philip Guston, courtesy Hauser & Wirth. Photo: courtesy Collection Stedelijk Museum Amsterdam – Figures 12, 19: © Georg Baselitz 2019. Photo: © bpk / Bayerische Staatsgemäldesammlungen – Figures 14, 17: Chaïm Soutine © VG Bild-Kunst, Bonn 2019 – Figure 18: © The Willem de Kooning Foundation, New York / VG Bild-Kunst, Bonn 2019. Photo: © 2017 Christie's Images Limited – Figure 20: © Gerhard Richter 2019 – Figure 22: © Succession Picasso / VG Bild-Kunst, Bonn 2019 / © FABA Photo: Marc Domage – Figure 24: © The Andy Warhol Foundation for the Visual Arts, Inc. / VG Bild-Kunst, Bonn 2019 – Figure 26: Rainer Fetting © VG Bild-Kunst, Bonn 2019.

© 2020, Théo de Luca and
Koenig Books, London
Interviews © Théo de Luca

All rights reserved. No part of this publication may be reproduced, stored in a retrieval system or transmitted in any form or by any means, electronic, mechanical, photocopying, recording or otherwise, without the prior permission of the copyright holders and the publisher.

Editor: Théo de Luca
Design: Apolline de Luca

First published by Koenig Books, London

Koenig Books Ltd
At the Serpentine Gallery
Kensington Gardens
London W2 3XA
www.koenigbooks.co.uk

Printed in Europe

Distribution
Germany, Austria, Switzerland / Europe
Buchhandlung Walther König
Ehrenstr. 4,
Deutschland - 50672 Köln
Tel: +49 (0) 221 / 20 59 6 53
verlag@buchhandlung-walther-koenig.de

UK & Ireland
Cornerhouse Publications
Ltd. - HOME
2 Tony Wilson Place
UK – Manchester M15 4FN
Tel: +44 (0) 161 212 3466
publications@cornerhouse.org

Outside Europe
D.A.P. / Distributed Art
Publishers, Inc.
75 Broad Street, Suite 630
USA - New York, NY 10004
Tel: +1 (0) 212 627 1999
orders@dapinc.com

ISBN 978-3-96098-742-0